Get It Together

Math Problems for Groups Grades 4–12

Tim Erickson

Curriculum Developers   Bill Finzer
Lynne Alper
Paul Giganti
Sherry Fraser
Kay Gilliland
Gary Tsuruda

Wordsmiths   Ruth Cossey
Jean Stenmark
Nancy Kreinberg

Illustrator   Rose Craig

Cover Artist   Sally Noll

 Lawrence Hall of Science
Berkeley, California

The Lawrence Hall of Science is a public science center, teacher inservice institution, and research unit in science and mathematics education at the University of California at Berkeley. For many years, it has developed curricula and teaching strategies to improve mathematics, science, and computer education at all levels, and to increase public understanding of those areas.

For information and additional copies, contact:

EQUALS
Lawrence Hall of Science #5200
University of California
Berkeley, CA 94720-5200

(800) 897-5036
(510) 642-1910
(510) 643-5757 (Fax)

Website: www.lawrencehallofscience.org/equals
Email: eqs_pubs@uclink4.berkeley.edu

EQUALS gratefully acknowledges support in preparing this publication from the Carnegie Corporation of New York. Any opinions, conclusions, or recommendations expressed in this book are those of the authors and do not necessarily reflect the views of the Carnegie Corporation.

Printing (last digit): 19 18 17 16 15 14 13

ISBN 0-912511-53-2

Contents

> This middle section contains what we call *families* of problems for groups, and is occasionally interrupted by a couple pages of advice. Look on the next two pages for an expanded listing of the problem families and the advice they surround.

More Contents

In this table, the problem families themselves are on the right; other sections—including the "advice"—are listed on the left.

Preface

EQUALS is a teacher education program at the Lawrence Hall of Science in Berkeley, California. EQUALS helps elementary, secondary, and post-secondary educators acquire methods and materials to attract female and minority students to mathematics, and to encourage their interest in math-based fields of study and work. Since 1977, EQUALS has provided from 10 to 60 hours of inservice for over 44,000 teachers and educators nationwide. EQUALS also has five sites throughout California, ten national sites, and enthusiastic representatives in Australia, New Zealand, Sweden, and Costa Rica.

We have long believed that we should teach mathematics well to everyone, and that teaching many different areas of mathematics is an important component of teaching well. We also believe in breaking the mold of the teacher standing in the front of the classroom ("I taught it to them, but they didn't learn it."). One way to do that is to let the students work together in groups.

We at EQUALS believe in cooperative learning, fervently. We believe that learning in groups is an opportunity for real improvement in education, not just another fad. We believe that we should work to develop social skills as well as academic skills in every discipline. Most important, we believe that cooperative learning holds additional promise that every student will have an opportunity to perform at her or his maximum potential in mathematics and not be restricted by the expectations of peers, teachers, parents, society, or self.

To make it work, though, teachers need good materials. Here is our offering. *Get It Together* is a collection of math problems for groups created in response to requests by teachers attending EQUALS workshops. We got the idea for these problems from the Humboldt County (California) Green Box materials, in which they were called "Six Bit" problems. We have maintained their format, and are greatly in their debt. We introduced them to our teachers as "cooperative logic" problems. They have been great favorites. They seem to be an easy way for teachers to begin to use groups in their classrooms, as well as good problems for classes experienced in group work.

These problems are not all there is to cooperative learning. They are only one type of experience. Many educators and researchers, some of which are acknowledged on page 177, have devoted their professional lives to cooperative learning. Like Newton, we stand "on the shoulders of giants." We are especially indebted to the careful and humane thinking of Ruth Parker and Laurel Robertson. In addition, many EQUALS teachers have come back to us with glowing stories of success with cooperation in their classrooms and thoughtful suggestions for what works best and what we should present to the teachers who come to us. Of these, Joan Sung has been especially helpful and inspirational.

We received a great deal of help producing *Get It Together*. A group of teachers got together in 1987 to brainstorm possibilities for the book and to give us advice. They were Barbara Bankovitch, Dianne Barrows, Heidi Boley, Bev Braxton, Joan Carlson, Jan Dougall, Diane Downie, Bill Finzer, Harvey Garn, Kathi Griffen, Sr. Maureen Hally, Meg Holmberg, Deborah Kitchens, Linda Lipner, Bill Medigovich, Diane Meltzer, Suzy Ronfeldt, Gary Tsuruda, Molly Whiteley, and Bob Whitlow. At that meeting, Gary showed us his Polygons, one group came up with the idea for the Martian problems, and another designed the *Number Shapes* family. Joe Brulenski helped develop some of the spinners problems. There were many more terrific ideas, of course, and excellent criticism of some of our early efforts. Mattye Pollard-Cole was with us in spirit; she and her colleagues in Colorado relentlessly field-tested more activities as we created them and gave valuable feedback. We are greatly indebted to all of these people who were so generous with their time and creativity.

A small army of EQUALS and MATHTEQ participants helped us field-test these activities once they were created. They included: Toby Alexander, Charlene Arbogast, Keith Barton, Ruthanne Bexton, Lynn Biddinger, Dee Bond, Diane Bredt,

Susan Butsch, Deborah Casey, Carol Chamberlain, Elizabeth Dallas, Jan Dougall, Amy Edgerley, James Friedrich, Donna Glassford, Nels Gonsalves, Caryn Gregg, Sarah Hall, Tom Hall, Becky Hemann, Beverly Hodge, Edna Hom, Bob Houghteling, Jody Jackson, Jean Jay, Jerrilyn Kaplan, Diane Kaz, Clarice Key, Marsha King, Cheryl Kleinschmidt, Ann Kyle, Athena Leonard, Jamila Makini, Linda Miller, Debbie Molov, Lynn Mooney, Cindy Motsinger, Thelma O'Brien, Mary Olthoff, Amy Parker, Anna Payne, Jane Peterson, Laurie Porter, Lisa Quintella, Carol Roach, Barbara Robisin, Linda Scott, Alfred Sisk, Steven Smith, Kim Straughn, Judy Sullivan, Gale Sunderland, Marge Tapia, Janet Teel, Barbara Tocher, Teresa Tocher, Judy Vincent, Martha Vlahos, Alice Wallace, Eric Watterud, Loudd Webster, Susan Wilkinson, Teresa Wong, David Woodford (aka Woody), and Bertha Yanez. If we missed anyone, we apologize!

There are a few other contributors who deserve mention. Bay Area Science Project participants found an elusive mistake. Charles Baker, a long-time friend of mine, once suggested the names Rooda and Stooda that appear in one problem. Bob Whitlow invented Foofie the Glork, though Foofie's eponymous condo from this book is not exactly what Bob had in mind. Closer to home, Meg Holmberg and Anne Erickson kept me well-supported and mostly sane, respectively, through the difficulties that befall any large project. Meg also made valuable suggestions on the writing, and Anne brought me Play-Doh, crayons, or Dr. Seuss books when I needed them most.

Most of the work, though, beginning with years of experience with this kind of problem and countless hours of careful thought and conversations about what was important, all the way through initial testing of the new problems and specific comments about this manuscript, was put in by EQUALS and FAMILY MATH staff members: Lynne Alper, Sue Arnold, Mary Jo Cittadino, Ruth Cossey, Karin Duval, Sherry Fraser, Paul Giganti, Kay Gilliland, Helen Joseph, Nancy Kreinberg, Harriet Nathan, Jean Stenmark, Virginia Thompson, and Linda Witnov.

How We Made This Book

Get It Together represents our second foray into large-scale desktop publishing, and our most complex. The book has been designed and laid out entirely on Macintosh computers, some of which were donated by Apple Computer, Inc. Only the cover was produced using "traditional" methods. Text was written using Microsoft Word 3.02; we produced problem pages in MacDraw II from Claris Corporation. The illustrations began as pen and ink, and were scanned using an Apple scanner at 300 dpi and modified (in what we sometimes called the "digital diversity project") using Image Studio, a high-resolution image processing program from Letraset. To do the layout, we combined all of these elements with PageMaker version 3 from Aldus. The resulting document took up most of sixty megabytes of disk space. Most of that was art. We printed page proofs on a LaserWriter II NTX (anything less couldn't handle the memory demands of the art files). UC Printing produced the final pages using a Linotronic 100 imagesetter at 1270 dpi. Those were photographed directly to make the plates. The heads are ITC Avant Garde; the body text is mostly Palatino.

Many people helped with the technical side: Ron Bannister and Sue Sheehan of UC printing patiently helped us solve seemingly intractable technical problems; Jenny White lent us the Mac II whose speed made timely layout possible; and Carol Turnbull helped us by scanning the original art and arranging for us to use the NTX. The biggest thanks, though, go to Celia Stevenson, whose expertise with all of these programs and "don't worry, be happy" attitude enabled me to stew over the words while she did hundreds of necessary but unexciting jobs like creating the problem index, adjusting page numbers, and making changes marked in proofs.

Tim Erickson
Berkeley, California
March, 1989

Introduction

You're holding in your hands a collection of math problems from the EQUALS program at the Lawrence Hall of Science (University of California at Berkeley). The problems span grades 4–12, include a wide range of mathematics topics, and are presented in a special format. They are problems for groups, not individuals, to solve together.

Each problem is in the same format: the information a group will need to know has been put on clue cards. Each member of the group will have a different bit of information, so everyone will have to cooperate to solve the problem. This particular format for group problems—though not the alpha and omega of cooperative tasks—is an especially easy one for teachers to begin with in mathematics.

Cooperation, Equity, and Math Learning

When we introduce problems like these to students, we explain the rules, and focus on the idea that their *groups* will have problems to solve. Then the groups get to work. They get pretty excited. After we've done a few problems, we stop and talk about what it was like to do math problems this way.

Everybody has a part to do is the first thing they say. That's the biggest benefit from an equity point of view. When teachers talk, many students stop paying attention. When students are in a group, they are almost always engaged.

It's easier with many brains is another typical comment. True. Chances are that somebody else sees things we don't.

I saw someone else work the problem a different way is another observation students make. There are many ways to solve a problem; we may gain insight into mathematical models that will help us beyond this one problem.

The group used a lot of math words in the discussion. Using mathematical language is more significant than a simple vocabulary drill. "Talking math" helps us cement our understanding of the mathematics behind the terms.

We knew when we were right. When students are doing the problems, we tend not to tell groups if their answers are right, and we don't answer questions unless everybody in the group agrees they need help. Working in a group fosters independence in learning. Students realize that the teacher is not the sole source of knowledge. Peers can explain things and assess whether they've done it right or not.

Some aspects of cooperative learning benefit the teacher as well:

There are fewer "units" to supervise. Instead of thirty-two students, you will have eight groups. That means you are more free to encourage groups who confront really perplexing problems.

The teacher can spend more time watching the students. As you circulate around the room, you will see the students solving problems. Because they become self-sufficient (or maybe group-sufficient) there will be more time for you to observe; you'll have a better chance of finding out what they're really thinking.

The result of all this is pretty rosy; we can go on:

- Doing group work as well as lecture and seat work appeals to more modalities; if we're interested in equity, we'll want to try to offer as many different ways of learning as possible.

- Problems like these can open the door to including other disciplines in the math class-room, thereby integrating the curriculum. This will also help underserved students by appealing to more interests and showing that math might be important outside of math class.

- Another regular outcome of these problems is success. Groups do *solve* these problems; often problems much more complex than individuals in the group could solve. This success can be a great boost to morale—theirs and yours.

- All students—from the most gifted to the slowest—benefit from learning to explain themselves more clearly and concisely.

- You may observe "weak" students being effective and contributing group members, and "strong" students may discover that they can get in the way of their group's solution.

- Learning to work together is important in itself. Most jobs require it, though it doesn't seem to be taught explicitly anywhere. Nowhere is this more true than in math-related fields.

Cooperation in the math classroom helps us advance several goals as we provide good, equitable mathematics education. We want to put students in genuine problem-solving situations, and to observe students working on problems so we can assess what they really understand. We want problems to be complex but not intractable, and we want students to persist and succeed. We want to help students become autonomous learners, independent of the teacher and free of pat answers.

We hope students will make mathematics their own, talking math and building understanding by solving problems with others. We hope they will be flexible and have access to many strategies, that they will see that mathematics is not an activity undertaken in isolation. Mathematics demands working together and listening as well as raw analytical prowess. All of these goals—every single one—are advanced by students working together effectively in groups.

Assessment

How do you assess cooperative lessons? Assessment will have to change: tests alone won't tell the story. And you must assess yourself and the lesson as well as the students and the groups.

There are many strategies for getting rich information from groups and individuals about what they understand—both about mathematics and about the social aspects of cooperation. In a section beginning on page 112, we'll talk about classroom observation and student writing as alternatives to traditional testing.

Getting Started

Choose which problems you want to do. Copy the problem pages and cut out the clues. Some pages have more than just clues. Each group receives an envelope with clue cards for one problem (and the other stuff) in it, at least one clue per group member. Any other material (blocks, beans, pencils, compasses, whatever) should be available.

Every problem in this book has the same structure and the same rules. Students need to learn the rules and the behavioral norms, which you should review frequently and display prominently.

The Rules

Each group should have an envelope to start with. When it's time to begin, open the envelopes, find the clue cards, and pass them out to members of the group.

When you get your clue, you may look only at your own clue. You may not look at anyone else's. You may share your clue by telling others what's on it, *but you may not show it to anyone else.*

If you have a question, you must check with your group first. If your group agrees that everyone has the same question, you may all raise your hands and the teacher will come.

Behavioral Norms

These may differ somewhat from classroom to classroom. Here are some we recommend.

- **Follow the rules of the activity.** These might include, no questions for the teacher unless everyone in the group agrees they don't know.

- **Make sure everybody gets to participate.** This may simply mean, everybody gets to talk; it may also mean, everybody gets to move the blocks. It may be up to your students to decide what that means in a particular situation.

- **Listen to what other people say.**

There are other beneficial norms you might introduce, depending on what your class needs:

- **Try to give reasons for what you say.** Everybody needs this, and it is a skill that is hard for students to learn.

- **Ask others for their opinions.**

- **Help others—without telling them what to do or giving answers.**

- **Get help if you need it.** And this help should come from the group first and the teacher last.

We are not so naïve as to believe that sitting students down in groups will make them autonomous learners. When you read every word in this book, and digest a few books or articles about cooperative learning, you'll have the impression that there are half a zillion different things to watch out for, explicitly stated or implied. Monday morning is coming and you want to try this. What should you think about?

Ensure a successful experience the first time.
Chances are your students have some group skills; they can start out on a problem in which the math is easy for them. Don't push it! You need to attend to the groups and not worry about the math. Check page 180 to get a good "Starter" that's appropriate to your grade level.

Decide what to watch for.
Pick something to do with social skills to observe in your class, so you can see what it's like to observe for cooperation in a math class. Maybe look to see if everybody gets a turn. Later, pick an academic behavior to look at as well.

Decide on a grouping strategy.
Don't let them choose their own groups. Live a little! Try random groups.

Prepare the materials.
Give yourself enough time to get things reproduced and cut ahead of time.

Prepare yourself
Read all of the problems you plan to do in class ahead of time, and solve some—with a small cooperative group, if possible, but alone if necessary. Stay alert to terms or concepts in the problems that may be new to your students. As you get more comfortable, you'll find you can give students problems you couldn't solve!

Explain the rules and expected behaviors.
Let students know how you expect them to behave in a group. We just listed the rules and some suggested behaviors on page 10. Check to see that students understand them.

Do it!
And when you do, try to remember three things: observe what you set out to observe; don't intervene for individuals, but try to interact with groups; and try not giving any answers. There is a long section called "Restraint" beginning on page 150.

Debrief the Class
Afterwards, ask them what happened. Don't tell them what you thought—let them do the talking. Ask questions, and listen carefully to the answers. Did they think everybody got a chance to talk? Did anybody learn something from a group member? What strategies did groups say they used to solve the problems? How did the groups decide they had the right answer? Make sure you call on as many different groups and individuals as possible.

Debrief yourself
As soon as you can get some time alone, sit down and think about what happened. Better still, think and write. You were watching for one social skill. What others occurred to you to watch next time? What are your class's strengths? Its weaknesses? How did they do on the math? Were any individuals disruptive? Were any individuals surprisingly competent? How did the random groups work out? Five minutes of reflection will pay back enormous dividends.

Our Favorite Grouping Strategies

We like heterogeneous, random, impermanent groups, with four students in them. We like the groups to last for longer than one class session, but not more than a couple weeks to a month. We like the idea of everybody working with everybody else. When someone objects to being in a group with Aloysius, we point out that anybody can work with anybody for two weeks.

We most often make random groups by counting off and dividing, but passing out playing cards works just fine (so the aces go to this table, the jacks over here, and so forth).

About the Problems

Now we're ready for the problems themselves. First we'll talk about how the problems are organized and how they look on the page. We'll even present a few sample problems as examples. The examples will be full-size, just like the other problems in this book, so you'll be able to reproduce them and use them with your students.

Later, you will read sections about problem-solving strategies (beginning on page 40), about manipulatives (page 42), about what can go wrong (page 74), the jigsaw technique (page 75), assessment (page 112), and about exercising self-restraint (page 150).

Families of Problems

We discovered, creating these, that problems tend to fall into "families." In general, problems in a particular family require similar types of solutions, involve a specific subject area in mathematics, or are appropriate to a particular grade level. Often the families have some problems at one grade level that are easier or much harder.

Problem families help you find problems you're looking for (but not always; browsing is a good idea). They also help you organize your work if you're trying to invent new problems. For example, it's easier to invent a problem that fits into an existing family than to create a new family.

We introduce each family with a page describing it, the areas of mathematics it covers, and particular attributes of these problems that distinguish them.

A blip. This one means the clue came from the middle on the left side of the page.

5. sozahap zillener

zik zillsozan rezirkhap marcoshpa

zu zill glin pook zu toba glin

How the Problems are Laid Out on the Page

We've tried to make the problems easy to use in a variety of situations. We've made some important choices about what appears on the problem pages.

- After you reproduce the page, cut along the dashed lines *and along the copyright line at the bottom of the page.* You can throw the bottom away. When you do that, the margins around all the boxes will be the same and the lines are more likely to line up if you use a paper cutter.

- Notice that every clue has a gray band with the name of the problem in it. All problems from the same family have the same shade of gray.

- The gray band at the top of each clue has a blip on one side or the other. Look at the *Cookie Crumbs* problem on the facing page and at the diagram at left. The blip can be either at the top, in the middle, or at the bottom of the band. *The position of the blip corresponds to the position of the clue on the original, uncut page.* Check that out. That means that if five copies of one problem get mixed up, you can sort them by clue without reading all of them.

- Most problems have *optional clues.* It's possible to solve the problems without them. If there are optional clues, they appear at the *bottom* of the page *and their blips are a different shade than the blips in the required clues.*

Cookie Crumbs

Rachel, Linda, and Eve were friends sitting in a circle on the grass.

Rachel passed three chocolate chip cookies to the person in blue.

Who wore which color?

Cookie Crumbs

Eve passed three macaroons to the person who passed her cookies to the person wearing green.

Who wore which color?

Cookie Crumbs

Each person passed three cookies to the friend on her left.

Who wore which color?

Cookie Crumbs

Rachel, Linda, and Eve were dressed in red, blue, and green, but not necessarily in that order.

Who wore which color?

Cookie Crumbs

The person who was wearing green did not get a macaroon.

Who wore which color?

Cookie Crumbs

The person wearing red passed along three oatmeal cookies.

Who wore which color?

Eve

Rachel

Linda

Blue

Green

Red

from *Get It Together* • EQUALS, Lawrence Hall of Science

More About the Problems

Even though all of the problems are in the same format, they come from widely different areas of mathematics and are appropriate to different ages of students. Besides those obvious differences, however, there are two other ways problems differ from one another—and from traditional problems: some have more than one solution, and some have "distributed questions."

Multiple solutions

As in life, some of these problems have more than one solution. We've tried to indicate which ones have multiple solutions. It's always possible your students will find others, or will interpret clues in novel ways to create still more. Often, a group will find a solution and believe that they've completely solved the problem. What you do with that depends on your goals.

- You may want to suggest from the beginning that students look for additional solutions when they have found one.

- You may want to let students go on after having found one solution, and never bring it up.

- You may want to probe the group when they finish a problem: "Is this the only solution to the problem?"

- You may want to let it pass in the work time but bring it up in the debriefing. "Let's hear the answers that your groups got for the Figs problem…" and let them discover that they got different answers while verifying that they had the same problem. Maybe the next time they can try to find *all* the solutions.

Distributed Questions

In some families, the question the group has to answer appears only on one or two of the clues. Holders of most clues don't even know what the question is! Attentive students quickly learn to ask, "who knows the question?" as soon as the clues are passed out. More fodder for debriefing.

In some problems, the group has to answer more than one question, and the questions are distributed among the clues. *B, G, & E* (page 146) is a particularly pathological example of this.

Optional Clues

In many of the problems, there are one or two optional clues. That doesn't mean the clues are useless, it's just that it's possible to solve the problem without those clues. In some cases, it's no more difficult with only four, in others it's substantially harder. The original reason for making these clues was to make it possible for groups of four, five, or six to use the problems.

There are two popular strategies for dealing with these clues. We like them both.

- Pass all the clues out. Some people will get two.

- Save out the optional clues and use them to help check. Either you or the students can find them and set them aside without reading them.

Labels

Many of the problems have manipulative labels besides clues. You may use these or not as you see fit. They are a different size than the clues so you can distinguish them without reading.

Some labels are meant to label a pile of counting manipulatives like beans. For example, if Martha has a certain number of kiwi fruit, you might use beans to represent kiwi fruit, and a label marked "Martha" to mark a place to put the beans.

Other labels can be the manipulatives themselves. If there are things to be placed in a certain order (the *Lineup Logic* family, beginning on page 88, is a good example), students can use labels with the names of those things to represent possible solutions.

Still other labels (like some in the *Mysteries* family) have shared information on them, like a clue for the whole group.

Students can make the labels themselves or you can give them the labels we have provided. It's your call. Labelmaking can be part of the problem-solving process; some of us are now seasoned label-makers and start tearing up sheets of paper and scribbling names at the drop of a problem statement.

Grade Level

It's hard to assign grade levels to these problems. We have produced a chart on page 180—the last page in the book—that gives a range of grade levels for each family based on our field tests. Within each family, problems may vary widely in difficulty; we've generally put easier problems first. But "easy" problems can be appropriate for older or very talented students, and "hard" ones can be accessible to younger students or those who are having trouble with math.

Management of Materials

One way to organize the clues and labels for these problems is to put them in labelled envelopes. Make enough envelopes of cut-out clues for the class, label them, and you have a class set that you can use from year to year and lend out to your colleagues. When a group finishes a problem, ask them to put the clues and labels back in the envelope; then you can give them a new one. If the envelopes stay on the table, you can tell at a glance which problems a group has done.

You have two routes to go with the manipulatives and the other tools—paper, pencil, rulers, compasses, and so forth. You might want to give each group the relevant material yourself, thus ensuring everyone has everything they need. As you and your students get used to working in groups, however, it will be easier on you—and better for them—if they get the materials and return them themselves. If you have group roles, only the runner (or gofer, or whatever) is allowed up to get new problems or materials, and no group can take more than it needs. The cleanup person is responsible for seeing that everything is put away at the end.

Tables for the groups and cubbyholes for individual books are best, but you may still have individual desks with hinged tops. If so, you might be able to push them together into semipermanent clusters of four or five, or you might have a place where students can meet on the floor. Maybe half the students can turn around (depending on the design of the chairs) to share others' desk surfaces. The important thing is to create some shared horizontal space where groups can work. The right equipment is great, but it's possible to create a cooperative classroom without it.

Hundred Chart Hunts

Concept Areas

Logic, process of elimination, inequalities, properties of numbers and multiples. Vocabulary: even, odd, difference, sum, digit, product, greater than, less than, not.

For Each Group:

- A hundred chart (on the facing page)

- At least 100 small manipulatives (like beans or pasta shells) to mark the mat.

Many teachers find it is easier to reproduce several mats per group and let students write on them with pencils or crayons.

Description

Each group needs to find a particular number on the hundred chart. Individual clues either select or eliminate subsets of the whole chart, and range from very simple ("The number is even") to more complex ("The sum of the number's digits is greater than nine"). Students can mark the Hundred Chart with crayons or manipulatives to keep track of the group's deductions.

Features

Problems in this family are good starters for students of all ages. They have several things going for them:

- The questions are straightforward. Unlike some later problems, it is clear what the group's goal is in every problem—to find a particular number somewhere on the chart.

- The clues have no extraneous information.

- Every problem has a solution, and all of them have only one.

- Every problem makes good use of concrete materials—the mat and the manipulatives. It is usually easier to solve the problem with the mat than any other way.

Problems in this family are also excellent jigsaw problems (see the section on page 75 on using the jigsaw technique).

Possible Debriefing Questions

Did you need everybody's clue to solve the problem?

What patterns do you see on the chart for even numbers? Multiples of five? Multiples of three?

Do you put a bean (or a mark) on a number to show it's a possibility or to show that it has been eliminated?

Hundred Chart

1	2	3	4	5	6	7	8	9	10
11	12	13	14	15	16	17	18	19	20
21	22	23	24	25	26	27	28	29	30
31	32	33	34	35	36	37	38	39	40
41	42	43	44	45	46	47	48	49	50
51	52	53	54	55	56	57	58	59	60
61	62	63	64	65	66	67	68	69	70
71	72	73	74	75	76	77	78	79	80
81	82	83	84	85	86	87	88	89	90
91	92	93	94	95	96	97	98	99	100

Tim's Number

Tim's number is a multiple of three.

Help your group find Tim's number on the Hundred Chart!

Tim's Number

Tim's number is a multiple of five.

Help your group find Tim's number on the Hundred Chart!

Tim's Number

If you add the digits of Tim's number, you get an odd number.

Help your group find Tim's number on the Hundred Chart!

Tim's Number

Tim's number is odd.

Help your group find Tim's number on the Hundred Chart!

Tim's Number

If you multiply the digits of Tim's number together, you get an even number.

Help your group find Tim's number on the Hundred Chart!

Tim's Number

Tim's number is near the center of the chart.

Help your group find Tim's number on the Hundred Chart!

from *Get It Together* • EQUALS, Lawrence Hall of Science

Meg's Number

The sum of the digits of Meg's number is greater than ten.

Help your group find Meg's number on the Hundred Chart!

Meg's Number

The difference between the two digits of Meg's number is greater than three.

Help your group find Meg's number on the Hundred Chart!

Meg's Number

Meg's number is a multiple of seven.

Help your group find Meg's number on the Hundred Chart!

Meg's Number

The first digit of Meg's number is larger than the second.

Help your group find Meg's number on the Hundred Chart!

Meg's Number

Meg's number is not odd.

Help your group find Meg's number on the Hundred Chart!

Meg's Number

Both digits of Meg's number are even.

Help your group find Meg's number on the Hundred Chart!

from *Get It Together* • EQUALS, Lawrence Hall of Science

Paul's Number

Paul's number is not located on an edge or a corner.

Help your group find Paul's number on the Hundred Chart!

Paul's Number

Paul's number is not an even number.

Help your group find Paul's number on the Hundred Chart!

Paul's Number

The difference of the digits in Paul's number is three.

Help your group find Paul's number on the Hundred Chart!

Paul's Number

Paul's number is not a multiple of three, five, or seven.

Help your group find Paul's number on the Hundred Chart!

Paul's Number

Paul's number is less than fifty.

Help your group find Paul's number on the Hundred Chart!

Paul's Number

The sum of the digits in Paul's number is 11.

Help your group find Paul's number on the Hundred Chart!

© 1989 The Regents of the University of California

from *Get It Together* • EQUALS, Lawrence Hall of Science

Keisha's Number

Keisha's number is a multiple of three.

Help your group find Keisha's number on the Hundred Chart!

Keisha's Number

The sum of the digits of Keisha's number is even.

Help your group find Keisha's number on the Hundred Chart!

Keisha's Number

Keisha's number is the *largest* number on the chart that fits all of the other clues.

Help your group find Keisha's number on the Hundred Chart!

Keisha's Number

Keisha's number is a multiple of five.

Help your group find Keisha's number on the Hundred Chart!

Keisha's Number

When you multiply the digits of Keisha's number together, you get an odd number.

Help your group find Keisha's number on the Hundred Chart!

Keisha's Number

Keisha's number is larger than 50.

Help your group find Keisha's number on the Hundred Chart!

from *Get It Together* • EQUALS, Lawrence Hall of Science

Find the Number

Concept Areas

Logic, the process of elimination, logical connectors such as AND and NOT, inequalities, divisibility, types of numbers such as primes, palindromes, perfect and triangular numbers. One problem uses Greatest Common Divisor.

For Each Group:

- Paper and pencil.
- Calculator.

Description

Groups are trying to find a number as in the *Hundred Chart Hunts* family, but now the number will probably not appear on the hundred chart. Each individual clue helps the group narrow down the possible solutions. Some of the clues introduce or use more esoteric properties than in the previous family, such as whether the number is a prime, a palindrome, or a triangular number.

Other Comments

What if Marcy gets a card claiming that the number is a palindrome, and she doesn't know what a palindrome is? Sometimes we explain the number property on the card with the clue; sometimes we explain it on another card; and sometimes we don't explain it at all. Students will learn to rely on the members of their group when they can't help themselves. Remember: make sure everyone in the group agrees that they need help from outside the group before you give it.

Features

How do these problems differ from the *Hundred Chart Hunts*?

- The clues in this set are harder, using more difficult concepts.

- The range of answers is greater, not confined to the hundred chart.

- Most importantly, students have to impose their own order on the problem to solve it. We don't give them a structure.

Because of this lack of imposed structure, you will notice a greater variety of problem-solving methods when you talk with students afterwards. For example, they may still use the process of elimination ("So we knew it was less than 1000 and greater than 750…"), but might also use guess and check ("When we tried five, it was too small, so we tried six…") or even more sophisticated reasoning ("Since it had only three factors, it had to be a perfect square.").

Problems from this family are also good candidates for jigsaw; see the section on page 75.

Possible Debriefing Questions

Did anyone come across any words you didn't know?

Why do they call triangular numbers triangular?

Do you think you could decide on one clue that told you the most?

If we made a problem and the answer were 258, write down (or tell me) some clues you might give someone else.

Andrea's Number

The product of the digits of Andrea's number is 36.

What could Andrea's number be?

Andrea's Number

Andrea's number is prime.

What could Andrea's number be?

Andrea's Number

Andrea's number is less than one thousand.

What could Andrea's number be?

Andrea's Number

Andrea's number is the *largest* number that satisfies all of the other conditions.

What could Andrea's number be?

Andrea's Number

One less than Andrea's number is divisible by five.

What could Andrea's number be?

Andrea's Number

One more than Andrea's number is divisible by 6.

What could Andrea's number be?

from *Get It Together* • EQUALS, Lawrence Hall of Science

Alexander's Number

Alexander's number is a palindrome, and the second and third digits are different.

Help your group find out what Alexander's number could be.

Alexander's Number

Alexander's number is prime and it's greater than one hundred.

Help your group find out what Alexander's number could be.

Alexander's Number

Alexander's number is odd, and the difference between the largest digit and the smallest digit is five.

Help your group find out what Alexander's number could be.

Alexander's Number

Alexander's number is less than one thousand, and the sum of its digits is 14.

Help your group find out what Alexander's number could be.

Alexander's Number

Alexander's number is not divisible by three, and it is less than 500.

Help your group find out what Alexander's number could be.

Alexander's Number

Alexander's number is a whole number with only two divisors: itself and one.

Help your group find out what Alexander's number could be.

© 1989 The Regents of the University of California

from *Get It Together* • EQUALS, Lawrence Hall of Science

Natalie's Number

Natalie's number is a palindrome. That means it reads the same forwards as backwards.

What could Natalie's number be?

Natalie's Number

Natalie's number is greater than ten thousand.

What could Natalie's number be?

Natalie's Number

Natalie's number has only one factor besides itself and one.

What could Natalie's number be?

Natalie's Number

Natalie's number is less than twenty thousand.

What could Natalie's number be?

Natalie's Number

The square root of Natalie's number is a palindrome. That means it reads the same forwards as backwards.

What could Natalie's number be?

Natalie's Number

The product of the digits of Natalie's number is zero.

What could Natalie's number be?

from *Get It Together* • EQUALS, Lawrence Hall of Science

Julian's Number

Julian's number is an abundant number. That means that the sum of all its factors (itself not included) is greater than itself.

What could Julian's number be?

Julian's Number

Julian's number is less than 200.

What could Julian's number be?

Julian's Number

Julian's number has only two distinct prime factors, though both of them are repeated.

What could Julian's number be?

Julian's Number

Julian's number is the square of a positive integer.

What could Julian's number be?

Julian's Number

The product of the digits of Julian's number is an even number.

What could Julian's number be?

Julian's Number

Julian's number is the sum of two adjacent triangular numbers.

There are at least two right answers to the question your group has to answer!

from *Get It Together* • EQUALS, Lawrence Hall of Science

Alma's Number

Alma's number has only one prime factor that's greater than twelve—and that factor occurs only once.

What's Alma's number?

Alma's Number

Three is the largest number that is a factor of both 495 and Alma's number.

What's Alma's number?

Alma's Number

94 is the largest factor Alma's number has in common with 188.

28 is the second perfect number.

What's Alma's number?

Alma's Number

The remainder you get when you divide Alma's number by seven is the same as the one you get dividing Alma's number by ten.

What's Alma's number?

Alma's Number

One of the factors of Alma's number is perfect, but that factor is not a prime.

Alma's number is a palindrome.

What's Alma's number?

Alma's Number

A perfect number's factors (excluding itself but including the number one) add up to itself.

The product of the digits of Alma's number is 32.

What's Alma's number?

from *Get It Together* • EQUALS, Lawrence Hall of Science

Kids With Stuff

Concept Areas

Algebra. The concept of a variable. Sums of unknowns. Solution of simultaneous equations using manipulatives.

Two of these problems have multiple solutions. They are clearly marked and include suggestions of how to handle them. Real-world problems seldom have one right answer; it's good to learn that can happen in math class as well.

Other Comments

Problems like these can be important experiences that will help prepare students for high school algebra. This can be valuable practice to cement the notion of a variable, demonstrate the value of manipulatives, and show that abstract x's and y's are not always the best tools to solve problems. The concept of a variable is central to much of higher mathematics and computer science; here we represent it simply and concretely as a number of beans next to a label.

For Each Group:

- Labels that you will cut from each sheet of clues. Include them in the problem envelopes.

- At least two kinds of manipulatives.

We often use blocks and beans. Other possibilities include: dry pasta, paper clips, dice, chips, and metal washers.

Students will benefit from working with beans and labels to represent problem solutions a few times before turning them loose on these. Older students (and many adults) will tend to try to use algebra. These are examples of problems more easily solved with beans and blocks than with abstraction.

Description

Each problem describes a number of kids with varying numbers of things. Each clue helps the group figure out who has how many. For example, your clue might tell you that Ferdinand and Imelda have 8002 shoes between them. Students can use manipulatives to represent possible values for the quantities to be found.

Students often put manipulatives next to labels—either ones we provide or ones they make themselves. They can modify solutions to the problems by moving manipulatives back and forth between the labels and referring to their clues.

Possible Debriefing Questions

What strategies did you use on these problems?

Did the manipulatives help?

How did you use them?

How did it feel when you found out that the problem had more than one answer?

What did you do when you got stuck?

Two kids With Animals

Each kid has the same total number of animals (when you add their pigs and chickens together).

How many pigs does Ronald have?

Two kids With Animals

Nancy's animals have — altogether — two more legs than Ronald's.

How many pigs does Nancy have?

Two kids With Animals

Ronald's animals have twelve legs altogether.

How many chickens does Ronald have?

Two kids With Animals

The two kids own three chickens between them. The rest of their animals are pigs.

How many chickens does Nancy have?

Two kids With Animals

Ronald has the same number of pigs as chickens, but Nancy does not.

Manipulatives might help you solve the problem.

Two kids With Animals

If Nancy gave Ronald a chicken, her animals would have only twelve legs in all.

There are four questions for your group to answer.

Ronald

Nancy

© 1989 The Regents of the University of California

from *Get It Together* • EQUALS, Lawrence Hall of Science

Four Kids With Beans

Kris and Moira together have nine beans.

How many beans does each kid have?

Four Kids With Beans

If Jay and Moira put their beans together, they'd have eleven beans.

How many beans does each kid have?

Four Kids With Beans

Erin and Jay have sixteen beans when you put their beans together.

How many beans does each kid have?

Four Kids With Beans

The four kids have a total of 25 beans. Kris and Jay, together, have the same number as Erin.

How many beans does each kid have?

Four Kids With Beans

Kris and Erin have a total of fourteen beans between them.

How many beans does each kid have?

Four Kids With Beans

No two kids have the same number of beans; Erin and Moira have fifteen together.

How many beans does each kid have?

Kris   Erin   Jay   Moira

© 1989 The Regents of the University of California   from Get It Together • EQUALS, Lawrence Hall of Science

Four Kids With Figs

Lalania and Nick have seven figs when you put theirs together.

How many figs does each kid have?

Four Kids With Figs

Lalania and Maurice have five figs when you put all their figs together.

How many figs does each kid have?

Four Kids With Figs

If Nick and Olivia put all their figs together, they'd have twelve.

How many figs does each kid have?

Four Kids With Figs

If Olivia and Maurice put all their figs in one basket, the basket would have ten figs.

How many figs does each kid have?

Four Kids With Figs

If the four kids put all their figs together and shared them equally, they'd each get four, but there would be one fig left over.

Use manipulatives to help you.

Four Kids With Figs

Don't pass this card out! This problem has multiple solutions. Treat it specially; consider asking followup questions like the ones at the beginning of this section, including

OK, you found a solution. Good! Can you find another?

OR

Now that we all have solutions, let's share and see what we got. (Then students will see that they're different.)

Lalania   Maurice   Nick   Olivia

from *Get It Together* • EQUALS, Lawrence Hall of Science

Three Kids With Marbles

Xanthia and Wolfgang together have 306 marbles.

How many marbles does each kid have?

Three Kids With Marbles

Yvonne and Xanthia would have 503 marbles if they put their marbles together.

How many marbles does each kid have?

Three Kids With Marbles

Yvonne is the only kid with over 300 marbles, but she has fewer than 400.

How many marbles does each kid have?

Three Kids With Marbles

When Wolfgang writes the number of marbles he has, the last digit is a five.

How many marbles does each kid have?

Three Kids With Marbles

Wolfgang, Yvonne, and Xanthia (pronounce the X like a Z, as in xylophone) each have over 100 marbles. How many marbles does each kid have?

Three Kids With Marbles

Don't pass this card out! This problem has multiple solutions. Treat it specially; consider asking followup questions like the ones at the beginning of this section, including

OK, you found a solution. Good! Can you find another?

OR

Now that we all have solutions, let's share and see what we got. (Then students will see that they're different.)

Xanthia

Yvonne

Wolfgang

© 1989 The Regents of the University of California

from Get It Together • EQUALS, Lawrence Hall of Science

Three Kids With Fruit

Andi has lots of apples (more than a dozen, but less than a hundred) but no oranges and no pears. In fact, she has half the total number of fruit.

Brent and Claudia are there too; between them they have more pears than oranges.

How many of which fruits does each kid have?

Three Kids With Fruit

If Claudia had twice as many pears, she would have one more pear than Brent. And you know what? She's the only kid with oranges. Neither Andi nor Brent have any oranges at all.

How many of which fruits does each kid have?

Don't forget you can use manipulatives to help your group solve the problem.

Three Kids With Fruit

Andi has half the total number of fruit (apples plus oranges plus pears) that all the kids have. And she has no pears.

If Claudia shared her oranges equally with Andi, they would each wind up with two oranges.

How many of which fruits does each kid have?

Three Kids With Fruit

Brent has no oranges and Andi has all the apples. Still, Brent and Claudia have the same total number of fruit, when you add up their apples, oranges, and pears.

How many of which fruits does each kid have?

Three Kids With Fruit

If Andi shared her apples equally with her friends Claudia and Brent and herself, there would be none left over.

Claudia has some pears. In fact, if she had twice as many as she has now, she would have one more pear than Brent.

How many of which fruits does each kid have?

Three Kids With Fruit

Claudia and Brent have the same total number of fruit (apples plus oranges plus pears).

And if they put just their pears together, they could not divide them equally — three ways — among themselves and Andi.

How many of which fruits does each kid have?

Claudia | Brent | Andi | Pears | Oranges | Apples

from *Get It Together* • EQUALS, Lawrence Hall of Science

Number Shapes

Concept Areas

Algebra. Solving simultaneous equations using manipulatives, this time in symbolic number sentences.

For Each Group:

- The number shapes mat from the facing page.

- Manipulatives for the students to place on the mat to represent the solution. The manipulatives should be relatively small, so they can fit. The biggest number in any solution is ten.

Description

These problems are abstract, using shapes—squares, triangles, and stars—to represent numbers. Students can represent proposed solutions by placing beans on the mat, and then easily change their minds by moving the beans around. Ideally, each student becomes responsible for seeing to it that his or her equation is satisfied. When all the students agree, the problem is solved.

While the first two problems are accessible to students in early elementary school, the last is definitely a problem for middle school and beyond.

Other Comments

These problems help further students' understanding of variables.

In *Kids With Stuff*, students solved simultaneous equations that arise out of situations. This family is more abstract, so in that sense, harder. Yet students traditionally have more trouble with "word problems" than with traditional "technique" problems. So which of these sets should you do first?

Perhaps you should mix them. Word problems make you represent a concrete situation in the language of mathematics—they are problems in abstraction. When students learn techniques without a context—divorced totally both from situations and the meaning of the numbers—they can exhibit what may be the most damning set of skills: mastery of technique without the ability to abstract. They may do well in computation, but they can't think.

Note Well

There are only three regular clues and one optional for each of these. (There are only three shapes, so you can get a solution with three clues.) Some teachers let students use the extra, blank clues to make up their own.

Possible Debriefing Questions

Which did you find easier—these problems or the ones in *Kids With Stuff*? Why?

How did your group use the manipulatives?

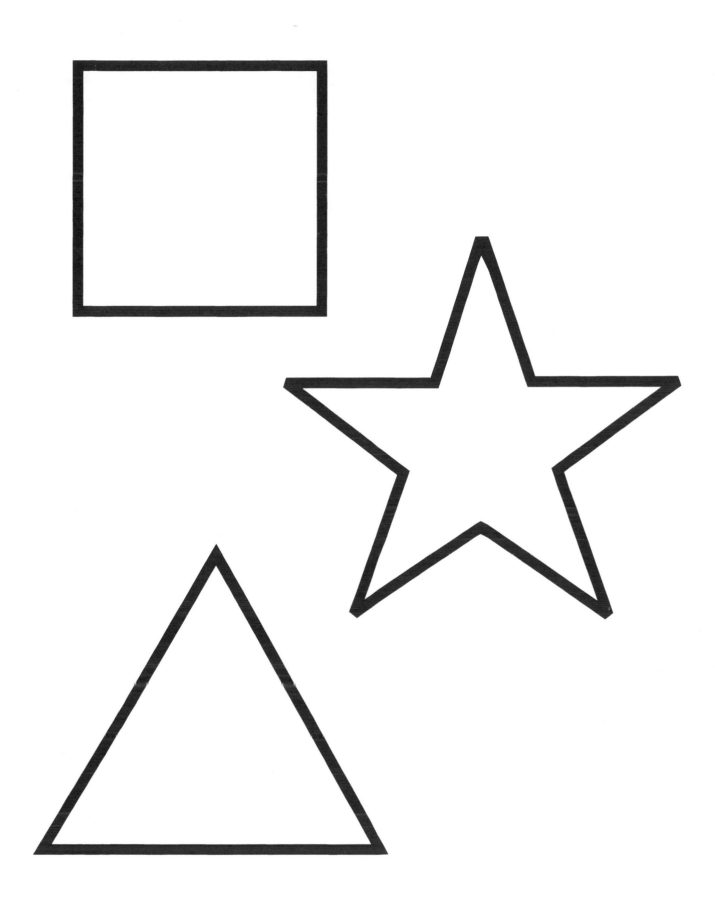

from *Get It Together* • EQUALS, Lawrence Hall of Science

Number Shapes 1

$$\triangle + \star = 3$$

Number Shapes 1

$$\star + \star = \triangle$$

Number Shapes 1

$$\triangle + \square = 6$$

Number Shapes 1

$$\square = 4$$

Number Shapes 1

Number Shapes 1

from *Get It Together* • EQUALS, Lawrence Hall of Science

Number Shapes 2

$$\bigstar + \triangle = 9$$

Number Shapes 2

$$\bigstar - \square = 2$$

Number Shapes 2

$$\square + \triangle = \bigstar$$

Number Shapes 2

$$\square + 1 = 6$$

Number Shapes 2

Number Shapes 2

from *Get It Together* • EQUALS, Lawrence Hall of Science

Number Shapes 3

$$\square + \square + \triangle = \star$$

Number Shapes 3

$$\triangle + 1 + \triangle = \square$$

Number Shapes 3

$$\square + \star + \triangle = 11$$

Number Shapes 3

$$\star - \square = 4 \times \triangle$$

Number Shapes 3

Number Shapes 3

from *Get It Together* • EQUALS, Lawrence Hall of Science

Number Shapes 4

$$3\bigstar + 1 = \square$$

Number Shapes 4

$$\square - 2\triangle = 2$$

Number Shapes 4

$$\frac{\triangle - 1}{\bigstar} = \frac{\square}{\square}$$

Number Shapes 4

$$2\bigstar + \triangle = \square$$

Number Shapes 4

Number Shapes 4

from *Get It Together* • EQUALS, Lawrence Hall of Science

Problem Solving

Students use the same problem-solving strategies in a group setting that they use as individuals. While this is not a book about problem-solving *per se*, it's worth a few pages to remember some of those important strategies and to point the way to other resources.

One such resource is Georg Pólya's *How To Solve It* (Doubleday, 1957), perhaps the grandfather of all problem-solving books. There are many others in many different styles.

But you can't learn problem solving by reading about it. You have to solve problems. Yet you can actually learn and use problem-solving strategies—they're not just buzzwords. Pólya, for example, suggests that if you can't figure out the problem as it is stated, create a simpler, related problem, and solve that. What does that mean? For one thing, if the problem has numbers, consider a similar problem with easier numbers. If a spatial problem is complicated and three-dimensional, see if it has an analog in two dimensions.

At the end of this section we present a list of strategies to start with. First, let's consider a few especially relevant ones.

Drawing Pictures or Diagrams

Virginia Thompson's father taught her to "draw a picture and write down everything you know." It was good advice. Drawing a diagram gives you a nonverbal representation of a problem. It helps you to visualize the situation, and it may reveal important relationships that are implicit in the problem statement. Labelling the figure is part of the process.

Guess and Check

We may cringe when our students "guess and check" because we want them to become analytical. But the students we most need to help may need to go through a phase of guessing and checking in order to develop some sense about the numbers in the problem. We can teach our students *not* to be haphazard in guessing and checking, but rather to try a reasonable number first, and then, when changing the trial numbers, to see whether the solution is getting closer or farther away.

Trying out a few numbers helps all students get the feel of the situation. Guess and check extends this all the way to a solution, and provides a workable fallback strategy if a fancier technique doesn't work.

Making Charts and Venn Diagrams

One way of organizing information is to make a chart or a diagram. Some charts record knowledge about what corresponds to what. Others, like maps or diagrams, show spatial relationships among elements of a problem. Timetables show temporal relationships. Sometimes making the right kind of chart just makes a problem open up and show you its solution.

Venn diagrams are a special kind of chart we use when we talk about sets. Certain kinds of problems are great for Venn diagrams. Here's one:

> At a meeting between sixty doctors and fifty architects, five-twelfths of all the women were doctors, and seven-twelfths of all the doctors were women. How many male architects were present?

Notice several things about this problem. First, the first time you read it, it sounds like doubletalk. That's a common property of word problems. A few more times through and you start to believe that you might be able to figure it out. But where to start? A Venn diagram helps. We have a whole family of problems that may use Venn diagrams beginning on page 82.

A List of Strategies

MOVE IT AROUND
    Act it out—role play
    Use manipulatives
    Sort or classify objects
    Measure it

PICTURE IT
    Close your eyes; visualize the problem
    Draw a picture or a diagram
    Use grids or arrays
    Make a tally or graph
    Look for patterns, similarities, differences

TAKE IT APART
    Break it into smaller problems
    Work backwards
    Look for key words (but be careful!)
    Figure out what you're trying to find
    Identify what you know already
    Identify extraneous information
    Figure out what other information you need

TRANSLATE IT
    Put it into your own words (paraphrase)
    Think of an earlier or easier problem
    Translate it directly into math symbols
    Put answers back into the problem to check

CONTROL IT
    Make a guess table
    Make a list
    Simplify (use smaller numbers)
    Estimate and predict
    Follow directions
    Check arithmetic computation
    Ask if it makes sense

AND...
    Do additional research
    Let your mind go (break set)
    Talk to other people, your partner, yourself
    Ask questions
    Use a calculator
    Sleep on it

Manipulatives

Manipulatives

Students of all ages can use manipulatives to advantage. Counters such as blocks, beans, or pasta shells should be available at all times. Older students (and their teachers) sometimes feel that blocks are kid stuff and that Real Mathematicians only use paper and pencil. But we all benefit from concrete materials. They help even advanced mathematicians see relationships in both spatial and numerical problems. In groups, manipulatives give the students something to talk about, something everyone can see and work with, a tool around which to organize their thinking.

It's pretty clear how important concrete materials can be for a spatial problem; the problem about the M&Ms on the facing page is a good example of a *numerical* problem that benefits from using manipulatives. Note the labels at the bottom of the page. You cut those out, and put them in the envelope with the clue cards. With more advanced students, you could omit the labels, and see if they make their own.

With the labels on the table, students can move manipulatives to the labels to represent proposed solutions or parts of solutions. If you think there are three tan M&Ms, put three beans next to "tan." As the group comes to understand the relationships among numbers in the problem, everyone can check the proposed solutions as new clues are read. And they can try different solutions simply by moving manipulatives around from label to label.

The "guess and check" strategy becomes elegant and concrete with manipulatives. The numbers of beans represent the values of variables; the labels are their names. The pencil-and-paper, x-and-y abstract version of variables is not for fourth-graders, but those same children *can* learn the concept of a variable and use it to solve a problem. They can do algebra.

M & Ms in a Bag

I have the most of Browns—seventeen—and the least of Tan M&Ms.

How many M & M's of each color do I have?

M & Ms in a Bag

I have as many Brown M&Ms as Yellow and Orange put together.

How many M & M's of each color do I have?

M & Ms in a Bag

I have twice as many Green as Tan M&Ms and two more Yellow than Tan M&Ms.

How many M & M's of each color do I have?

M & Ms in a Bag

I have the same number of green and orange M&Ms.

How many M & M's of each color do I have?

M & Ms in a Bag

My Green and Tan M&Ms add up to 15.

How many M & M's of each color do I have?

M & Ms in a Bag

I have 49 M&Ms in my bag and they are Brown, Green, Orange, Yellow and Tan.

How many M & M's of each color do I have?

Green   Tan   Brown   Yellow   Orange

from *Get It Together* • EQUALS, Lawrence Hall of Science

Build It!

Concept Areas

Geometry and spatial reasoning in three dimensions, logic in a geometrical setting. Using vocabulary: cube, face, edge, side, touching, above, below, each, every.

For Each Group:

- Colored cubes. You can solve every problem in this family by using a subset of eleven cubes: two each of red, blue, yellow, green, and orange, and one purple.

Description

The group needs to build a small structure out of colored cubes. Each clue tells something about the structure, for example, "there is a red block below the green block," or "the two orange blocks share an edge." In some problems, students have to deduce what blocks they need from their clues. In one problem, each clue restricts its holder to touching only one color of block.

These problems are popular starters. They're fun, and the first few are pretty easy without being trivial.

Purpose

We could go on for pages about the importance of geometry as part of mathematics learning at all levels. Let's just make three points here:

- First, the clues use mathematical language and force problem-solvers to use words like "face" and "edge" to get their clues across to others. Furthermore, students get into good discussions about whether "below" means "below and next to."

  - Second, most geometry instruction is two-dimensional, yet we live in a 3D world. Learning to think in three dimensions is powerful and useful.

  - Third, incorporating math language and 3D thinking will help those students who will need it the most—the students who don't often play with toys that enhance spatial visualization

Possible Debriefing Questions

How would you make these problems more difficult?

Did you use any words that had more than one meaning to the group?

Which was your favorite problem? Why?

Build It #1

There are six blocks in all.

One of the blocks is yellow.

Build It #1

The green block shares one face with each of the other five blocks.

Build It #1

The two red blocks do not touch each other.

Build It #1

The two blue blocks do not touch each other.

Build It #1

Each red block shares an edge with the yellow block.

Build It #1

Each blue block shares one edge with each of the red blocks.

from *Get It Together* • EQUALS, Lawrence Hall of Science

Build It #2

There are six blocks in all, in a tower six blocks high.

There is a yellow block on top.

Build It #2

The red block is above the green block.

Build It #2

One of the yellows is above the green block; the other is below it.

Build It #2

Each of the blue blocks shares a face with the green block.

Build It #2

No two blocks of the same color touch each other.

Build It #2

There are two yellows, two blues, one green, and one red in the set of blocks.

from *Get It Together* • EQUALS, Lawrence Hall of Science

Build It #3

There is a red block directly below a yellow block.

There is a green block on the bottom level.

Build It #3

There is a red block directly on top of a yellow block.

The highest block is on the third level.

Build It #3

There are six blocks in all.

An orange block shares a face with a green block and two others.

Build It #3

A blue block shares a face with a yellow block.

There is a red block on the bottom level.

Build It #3

A blue block touches red and green blocks only along edges.

There are three blocks on the bottom level.

Build It #3

A yellow block touches an orange block only along an edge.

from *Get It Together* • EQUALS, Lawrence Hall of Science

Build It #4

Special Rule:
you may only touch the orange block.

Each yellow block is above a red block; every red block shares an edge with the blue block.

Build It #4

Special Rule:
you may only touch yellow blocks.

Your clue: the one red block shares a face with the orange block.

Build It #4

Help build it with blocks, but the blue block is the only one you are allowed to touch.

Your clue: the green block shares a face with one of the two yellow blocks.

Build It #4

Your job is to help the group build it, but the green block is the only one that you are allowed to touch.

The blue block shares a face with the orange block and two others.

Build It #4

You may only touch the red block.

The highest blocks (neither of which are blue) are on the third level.

Build It #4

Don't pass this one out —these are instructions to the teacher!

Note that each player can touch only one color of block; if you don't use the optional clue, no one can touch red. That's intentional!

Minimum blocks: One blue, green, orange, red; two yellows.

from *Get It Together* • EQUALS, Lawrence Hall of Science

Build It Between

The green cube is between the orange cube and the yellow cube.

Build this row of six cubes!

Build It Between

The red cube is between the purple cube and the green cube.

Build this row of six cubes!

Build It Between

The orange cube is between the green cube and the red cube.

Build this row of six cubes!

Build It Between

The blue cube is between the green cube and the yellow cube.

Build this row of six cubes!

Build It Between

The yellow and the purple cubes are not between any cubes.

Build this row of six cubes!

Build It Between

Every cube is a different color from the others.

Build this row of six cubes!

from *Get It Together* • EQUALS, Lawrence Hall of Science

Stick Figures

Concept Areas

Geometry and the measurement of geometrical quantities such as perimeter and lengths of sides using nonstandard units (sticks). Vocabulary: regular and irregular polygons, equilateral and isosceles triangles, quadrilaterals, perimeter, vertex, base, congruent.

For Each Group:

- Each group should have at least fifteen sticks. They can be toothpicks, popsicle sticks, pencils, stirrers, whatever. They should all be the same length.

- A dictionary should be available.

Description

The group will make a geometrical construction out of sticks. Each group member gets a clue that says something about the solution, such as, "one triangle has a perimeter of seven sticks." The fifth problem is tricky; you have to break your mindset (but not a stick) to solve it.

Some of the problem solving requires clear spatial reasoning and exhaustive searches of all possibilities. For example, while there are two ways to make a triangle out of seven sticks without overlapping, there's only one way with six or five—and no ways to make one with four.

About *Sticks 5*: Don't Read This

We know you hate getting hints about the answers so skip this paragraph. Students will have trouble with *Sticks 5*. You should do the problem first in order to get an idea of what questions to ask to help them out. In case *you* run into trouble, here's an adult hint: it is impossible to make an isosceles triangle with a base of two and a perimeter of five without breaking sticks. It is not impossible to make *two* such triangles.

Other Comments

This set of problems seems harder than the *Build It* family that precedes it. What makes the difference? After all, these problems are only two-dimensional; those are three. Why do these seem more mathematical and less frivolous? Here is one possible reason:

The *language* in these problems is harder, though the concepts are not. *Edge* and *face* are more intuitive terms; while individuals may disagree, groups almost always come to agreement with the orthodox definition. In contrast, if no one in the group knows what *isosceles* or *regular* means, they may be stuck.

These problems are important because language is a filter. Our students need places to learn to use harder mathematical words with fluency so they can better understand the more abstract concepts that will require them.

Possible Debriefing Questions

Were there any problems with more than one solution? (*Sticks 2* is an example.)

How do you know your solution is the only one?

Did you learn any new words? Can you write about them in a new problem?

Stick Figures 1

There are twelve sticks in the figure. The sticks are unbroken and they don't overlap.

Make the figure!

Stick Figures 1

There are eight sticks in the square.

Make the figure!

Stick Figures 1

There are four sticks in the interior of the square.

All of the sticks are the same length.

Make the figure!

Stick Figures 1

There are six sticks in the triangle.

Make the figure!

Stick Figures 1

The triangle and the square share a side.

Make the figure!

Stick Figures 1

In the figure, both the rectangle and the triangle are regular polygons.

Make the figure!

from *Get It Together* • EQUALS, Lawrence Hall of Science

Stick Figures 2

There are fifteen sticks in all; the two triangles in the figure share a side.

Make the figure!

Stick Figures 2

The longest segment in the figure is two sticks long.

All of the sticks are the same length.

Make the figure!

Stick Figures 2

Both triangles in the figure are isosceles, but only one is equilateral.

Make the figure!

Stick Figures 2

The square shares a side with only one of the triangles.

Make the figure!

Stick Figures 2

Six of the sticks in the figure are in neither of the triangles.

Make the figure!

Stick Figures 2

The figure has two triangles and one square; all the sides are either one or two sticks long (no broken sticks!).

Make the figure!

from *Get It Together* • EQUALS, Lawrence Hall of Science

Stick Figures 3

There are twelve sticks in the figure. The sticks are unbroken and they don't overlap.

Make the figure!

Stick Figures 3

The figure is made up of two triangles that are not congruent.

Make the figure!

Stick Figures 3

One triangle has a perimeter of seven sticks.

Make the figure!

Stick Figures 3

No segment in the figure is shorter than two sticks.

Make the figure!

Stick Figures 3

The two triangles share a side.

Make the figure!

Stick Figures 3

There is a quadrilateral in the figure that has a perimeter of nine.

Make the figure!

from *Get It Together* • EQUALS, Lawrence Hall of Science

Stick Figures 4

There are eleven sticks in the figure. The sticks are unbroken and they don't overlap.

Make the figure!

Stick Figures 4

No sticks fall outside the pentagon.

Make the figure!

Stick Figures 4

All of the triangles are equilateral, but the pentagon isn't.

All of the sticks are the same length.

Make the figure!

Stick Figures 4

There are four triangles in the figure.

Make the figure!

Stick Figures 4

Each triangle shares sticks with two others.

Make the figure!

Stick Figures 4

One of the triangles is larger than the other three.

Make the figure!

© 1989 The Regents of the University of California

from *Get It Together* • EQUALS, Lawrence Hall of Science

Stick Figures5

There are ten sticks in the figure. The sticks are unbroken, and all are the same length.

Make the figure!

Stick Figures 5

The two triangles do *not* share a side.

Make the figure!

Some people think this problem is impossible, but it's not.

Stick Figures 5

Every isosceles triangle in the figure has a base two sticks long.

Make the figure!

Stick Figures 5

There are only two triangles in the figure, and they are congruent.

Make the figure!

Stick Figures 5

The two triangles share a vertex.

Make the figure!

Stick Figures 5

Each triangle has a perimeter equal to the length of five sticks.

Make the figure!

© 1989 The Regents of the University of California

from *Get It Together* • EQUALS, Lawrence Hall of Science

Pattern Blocks

Concept Areas

Geometry and logic, process of elimination, finding alternative solutions. Vocabulary: polygons, tessellation, vertex, rhombus, parallelogram, trapezoid, acute and obtuse angles, edge.

For Each Group:

- Pattern Blocks, available from educational supply places.

Description

Each group puts together a pattern based on the clues. Typical clues might be, "the pattern has the same area as seven yellow hexagons," or "there are twice as many triangles as trapezoids." Frequently, unusual words (such as *rhombus* or *tessellation*) get defined on some student's clue.

Most of these problems are *not* good starters because of vocabulary and subtleties in the problems. But students with experience with Pattern Blocks and other cooperative problems should do fine.

On the other hand, this is a good family for students to extend by making up their own problems. Consider having each group make up a pattern with four to eight pattern blocks—then create a cooperative problem for another group.

Features

These activities give students practice in spatial visualization and in the language of mathematics. They help all students understand more of mathematics by giving the practice both with spatial skills and the language that will help them communicate their understanding.

These problems can be difficult for some students because the clues often give information about a whole class of pieces rather than just one, as in, "every blue rhombus is touching two red trapezoids." That means you have to watch many pieces in the developing pattern instead of just one, and you have to be creative about finding alternative patterns that fit the clues.

Warning

Official Pattern Blocks come in six shapes with six different colors: yellow hexagons, orange squares, green triangles, red trapezoids, and different-shaped rhombuses in blue and white. If you have these shapes but not these colors, you should adapt the problems in this book before trying to use them!

Possible Debriefing Questions

Did anything surprise you in the way a pattern developed?

How did your group solve these problems? How did different people contribute?

Can you talk about different ways we use the word "pattern?" (in a quilt, in a behavior, etc.)

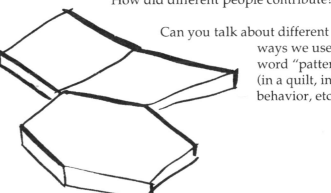

Left, Right, Middle, End

None of the Pattern Blocks in the row touch each other, and none of the shapes are congruent to any others in the row.

Make the row of Pattern Blocks.

Left, Right, Middle, End

The pieces at the ends of the row are not quadrilaterals, but there are two Rhombuses (Rhombi?!) in the middle of the row.

Make the row of Pattern Blocks.

Left, Right, Middle, End

The piece on the left has the largest number of acute angles of any piece. The piece on the right has more obtuse angles than any other.

Make the row of six Pattern Blocks.

Left, Right, Middle, End

The two pieces on the left end of the row are both regular—they have equal angles in every corner.

Make the row of six Pattern Blocks.

Left, Right, Middle, End

According to some math books, a rhombus has four equal sides. Though four Pattern Blocks have four sides, only three are rhombuses.

Make the row of Pattern Blocks.

Left, Right, Middle, End

The trapezoid is next to the piece that has the smallest angles.

Make the row of Pattern Blocks.

from *Get It Together* • EQUALS, Lawrence Hall of Science

Oh Hexagon

The area of this pattern is the same as four yellow hexagons.

Help your group make this pattern out of Pattern Blocks.

Oh Hexagon

There are only two kinds of pieces in this pattern—only two colors of Pattern Block.

Help your group make this pattern out of Pattern Blocks.

Oh Hexagon

There are six Pattern Blocks in this pattern.

Help your group make this pattern out of Pattern Blocks.

Oh Hexagon

The perimeter of this whole pattern is the same as the total perimeter of four separate green triangles.

Help your group make this pattern out of Pattern Blocks.

Oh Hexagon

There are the same number of pieces of each color in the figure.

Help your group make this pattern out of Pattern Blocks.

Oh Hexagon

There are four vertices (corners) in the *interior* of this figure.

Help your group make this pattern out of Pattern Blocks.

© 1989 The Regents of the University of California

from *Get It Together* • EQUALS, Lawrence Hall of Science

Terry's Triangle

The red and green pieces form two identical small triangles that are parts of Terry's triangle.

Use Pattern Blocks to help your group make Terry's triangle!

Terry's Triangle

The green piece that's right at the top of Terry's triangle doesn't touch the other green piece.

Use Pattern Blocks to help your group make Terry's triangle!

Terry's Triangle

There are twice as many blue pieces as green ones, and half as many reds as blues.

Use Pattern Blocks to help your group make Terry's triangle!

Terry's Triangle

There is a red piece right in the middle on the bottom of Terry's triangle.

Use Pattern Blocks to help your group make Terry's triangle!

Terry's Triangle

There are a total of eight red, green, and blue pieces in Terry's triangle.

Use Pattern Blocks to help your group make Terry's triangle!

Terry's Triangle

Each blue piece touches another blue piece.

Use Pattern Blocks to help your group make Terry's triangle!

from *Get It Together* • EQUALS, Lawrence Hall of Science

Glenda's Pattern

Glenda used only green, blue, red, and yellow Pattern Block pieces.

Help your group make Glenda's pattern!

Glenda's Pattern

No trapezoid shares a side with another trapezoid, but each trapezoid shares a side with the hexagon.

Help your group make Glenda's pattern!

✂

Glenda's Pattern

Each trapezoid, triangle and rhombus fit together to form a hexagon shape.

Help your group make Glenda's pattern!

Glenda's Pattern

Glenda used only one hexagon. The other eighteen Pattern Blocks are evenly divided among other shapes.

Help your group make Glenda's pattern!

Glenda's Pattern

Each rhombus shares only one vertex with the hexagon and one side with a triangle.

Help your group make Glenda's pattern!

Glenda's Pattern

You could cover Glenda's pattern with seven yellow hexagons.

Help your group make Glenda's pattern!

from *Get It Together* • EQUALS, Lawrence Hall of Science

Tessellate!

A tessellation is a pattern of identical shapes that cover a surface with no gaps and no overlaps, like floor tiles.

In this tessellation, each yellow hexagon touches three other yellow hexagons.

✂ ------------------------------------

Tessellate!

My tessellation is made up entirely of hexagons, but not all of the hexagons are yellow.

Use Pattern Blocks to make my tessellation!

Tessellate!

This tessellation uses yellow hexagons, blue rhombuses, red trapezoids, and green triangles.

Use Pattern Blocks to make my tessellation! Since it's infinite, you'll have to make only a part of it.

Tessellate!

In the tessellation, all of the non-yellow hexagons are made of three colors with the red trapezoid on top. You'll have to pick a direction for "top."

Use Pattern Blocks to make my tessellation!

Tessellate!

No rhombus touches any other rhombus; no triangle touches any other triangle.

Use Pattern Blocks to make my tessellation!

Tessellate!

It takes five Pattern Blocks to make one complete part (called a "unit cell") of this tesselation. You can make the whole pattern by repeating unit cells.

Use Pattern Blocks to make my tessellation!

© 1989 The Regents of the University of California

from *Get It Together* • EQUALS, Lawrence Hall of Science

Polygons

Concept Areas

Geometry of polygons. Vocabulary: area, perimeter, sides, right angle, parallel, congruent, interior angles, quadrilateral. Also, measurement using standard units such as inches and centimeters. Drawing to scale.

For Each Group

- Paper and pencil.
- Rulers.
- Protractors.

Note: there are only four clues to each problem.

Description

Each clue tells you something about the polygon the group has to draw. A student might read, "The longest side is two feet longer than the shortest side." This family extends the principles in the *Stick Figures* and *Pattern Blocks* families: we add measurement in traditional units—feet and centimeters instead of sticks; we add new concepts such as area and right angle; and we make the problems more abstract by making the group draw the figure instead of build it.

There are special problems that show up because of these features. Should students draw the polygons at actual size? Should they just estimate? What about *Polygon 3*, whose trapezoid is bigger than some kitchens? You may want to talk about drawing to scale.

Most of these problems are by Gary Tsuruda. Since he created them with four clues, we have left them that way. You may use the two blank clues any way you like—for example, to have groups write additional clues to go with their problems.

Features

Like those that precede it, this family gives students practice using the language of mathematics and it gives them important experiences translating descriptions in words into geometrical reality. It also cements the concept of a polygon.

Some students find these more abstract problems easier than the *Pattern Block* problems (page 56), possibly because they deal with only one polygon at a time. Yet the *Pattern Block* problems build a tactile base. All students need both the abstract and the concrete in order to succeed when it counts.

For more sophisticated problems in geometry, see the *Constructions* family that begins on page 126.

Possible Debriefing Questions

How did your group decide who was going to draw? Did you all get a chance to draw?

Did you draw the polygons at actual size?

Did you find any words you didn't know?

Polygon 1

This polygon has four sides.

Make the polygon!

Polygon 1

This polygon has four right angles.

Make the polygon!

Polygon 1

The length of this polygon is twice its width.

Make the polygon!

Polygon 1

The area of this polygon is eighteen square centimeters.

Make the polygon!

Polygon 1

Polygon 1

from *Get It Together* • EQUALS, Lawrence Hall of Science

Polygon 2

This polygon has only one right angle.

Make the polygon!

Polygon 2

The longest side is two feet longer than the shortest side.

Make the polygon!

Polygon 2

The third side—the one that is not longest or shortest—is one foot longer than the shortest side.

Make the polygon!

Polygon 2

This polygon has a perimeter of twelve feet.

Make the polygon!

from *Get It Together* • EQUALS, Lawrence Hall of Science

Polygon 5

Each side of this quadrilateral is congruent to one other side.

Make the polygon!

Polygon 5

The shortest side is half the length of the longest side.

Make the polygon!

Polygon 5

The two longest sides of this polygon meet in a 30° angle.

Make the polygon!

Polygon 5

This polygon has a perimeter of two feet.

Make the polygon!

NB: two solutions!

from *Get It Together* • EQUALS, Lawrence Hall of Science

Small City Blocks

Concept Areas

Logic and spatial orientation, the process of elimination, attributes of names, the use of NOT, compass directions, and "next-to" ness.

For Each Group:

- Labels that you will cut from each sheet of clues. Include them in the problem envelopes.

- Paper and pencil.

Note: there are only four clues for each problem.

Description

Each participant gets a clue to the arrangement of four houses on a small city block. The group has to arrange the houses on the block—one in each corner—and identify the names of the four streets that bound the block. To finish the problem, the clues instruct the group to make a drawing with their solution.

These are spatial logic problems; you'll meet several more in the *Lineup Logic* family. It's important to know that you really can deduce things about location from statements like, "Maria's house is not next to Marcus's." The manipulatives help students try out many different possible solutions and facilitate their finding the right one.

Features

In fact, the four problems are identical. Only the names and some orientations change from problem to problem. Therefore, you will *not* want to give one group a second set of clues when they finish a problem! (An exception would be if the fact that the problems are identical were the point of the lesson.)

Why are they identical? Two reasons. The first is that a teacher wanted to create a cooperative problem-solving event in a math olympiad, so needed problems that were as close as possible to the same difficulty. It may seem a little odd to create a cooperative math contest, but we obliged by creating these four problems. The second reason is to give an example of a relatively straightforward way to create new problems. There's a more extensive discussion of this later, on page 172. In case you want to try it, we've left you a blank template on page 73.

Possible Debriefing Questions

Did anything confuse you about the problems?

How did your group make the drawing—the map of the block?

What has to be on a map for it to be useful?

Small City Block A

Your answer has to have something on it that shows which way North, South, East and West are. For example, this would do:

North

West — East

South

Andrea does not live next to Cory.

Small City Block A

Your group's answer has to be a drawing showing the small city block, the four streets that surround it, and the four houses that are on it.

Oscar lives at the corner of Palm and Finch.

Small City Block A

In your drawing, you have to label all of the streets and all of the houses. Label each house with the name of the person that lives there.

All of the East-West streets in this town are named after trees (like Madrone); in fact, Madrone Street borders this small city block. And Andrea does not live on Hummingbird.

Small City Block A

The small city block is square. There are four houses, one in each corner. Each house is next to two other houses.

Katrina lives at the southeast corner of the small city block.

Palm

Madrone Street

Finch Street

Hummingbird

Andrea

Cory

Katrina

Oscar

from *Get It Together* • EQUALS, Lawrence Hall of Science

Small City Block B

Your answer has to have something on it that shows which way North, South, East and West are. For example, this would do:

Aimee does not live next to Charlotte.

Small City Block B

Your group's answer has to be a drawing showing the small city block, the four streets that surround it, and the four houses that are on it.

Duane lives at the corner of Plum and Elm

Small City Block B

In your drawing, you have to label all of the streets and all of the houses. Label each house with the name of the person that lives there.

All of the North-South streets in this town have names that begin with a vowel (like Oleander); in fact, Oleander Avenue borders this small city block. And Aimee does not live on Maple.

Small City Block B

The small city block is square. There are four houses, one in each corner. Each house is next to two other houses.

Brent lives at the northeast corner of the small city block.

Plum   Elm Street

Maple   Oleander Avenue

| Duane | Aimee | Charlotte | Brent |

from *Get It Together* • EQUALS, Lawrence Hall of Science

Small City Block C

Your answer has to have something on it that shows which way North, South, East and West are. For example, this would do:

Aaron does not live next to Boris.

Small City Block C

Your group's answer has to be a drawing showing the small city block, the four streets that surround it, and the four houses that are on it.

Annika lives at the corner of Taft and Strasburg.

Small City Block C

In your drawing, you have to label all of the streets and all of the houses. Label each house with the name of the person that lives there.

All of the North-South streets in this town have an even number of letters (like McKinley); in fact, McKinley Street borders this small city block. And Aaron does not live on Toyon.

Small City Block C

The small city block is square. There are four houses, one in each corner. Each house is next to two other houses.

Zoe lives at the southwest corner of the small city block.

Toyon

Taft Avenue

McKinley Street

Strasburg

Annika

Boris

Aaron

Zoe

from *Get It Together* • EQUALS, Lawrence Hall of Science

Small City Block D

Your answer has to have something on it that shows which way North, South, East and West are. For example, this would do:

Sybil does not live next to Tyrone.

Small City Block D

Your group's answer has to be a drawing showing the small city block, the four streets that surround it, and the four houses that are on it.

Roman lives at the corner of Lincoln and Diablo.

Small City Block D

In your drawing, you have to label all of the streets and all of the houses. Label each house with the name of the person that lives there.

All of the East-West streets in this town are named after U.S. Presidents (like Polk); in fact, Polk Street borders this small city block. And Tyrone does not live on Shasta.

Small City Block D

The small city block is square. There are four houses, one in each corner. Each house is next to two other houses.

Perryn lives at the northeast corner of the small city block.

Diablo

Polk Street

Shasta Way

Lincoln Avenue

Perryn   **Tyrone**   **Sybil**   **Roman**

from *Get It Together* • EQUALS, Lawrence Hall of Science

Small City Block

Small City Block

Small City Block

Small City Block

from *Get It Together* • EQUALS, Lawrence Hall of Science

What Goes Wrong

Even with your best planning, things can (and will) go wrong. No book will be able to describe to you the wide variety of imperfection you'll experience, but this will give you some idea.

Insincerity

Problem: you have observed that students are not very supportive of one another in their groups, so you explain that this time you'll be watching for encouraging behaviors. You elicit sample behaviors from the class, and it seems like they know what you're after. ("Good idea, Imelda!") But when you do the problems, the insincerity level is high, especially when you're near the groups.

This is understandable; the new "norm" of encouraging group members isn't internalized yet, so it still seems awkward. This phase may pass. On the other hand, it may be that the students are convinced that you're just counting encouragements and you don't mean it. Time for some discussion in debriefing. "Why do you suppose I was watching for encouraging today?" Or some clear message from you why you think encouraging is important.

Misinterpretation of Clues

Problem: students in one group misinterpret the clues in such a way that the problem becomes too hard, or too easy. Despite skillful probing questions, they still insist that they understand the problem.

If it only happens once, let them understand it their way. If it looks like it's going to happen repeatedly, plan in the debriefing to have different groups show how they solved the problems. Just as one confused member can get help from the group, a confused group can be set straight by the others. In any event, try to avoid just telling them they're wrong.

The Class Just Can't Do It

Problem: you give an apparently simple set of problems to students who ought to be well-prepared. It was supposed to be a warmup. But they get wrong answers and have a lot of trouble finishing in twice the time you thought it would take. They complain that they just don't get it.

This is one of the hardest "failures" to deal with. Sometimes, students are unprepared for these problems in ways we wouldn't expect. You need experience with spinners to do well with the spinner families. Students who don't understand multiples will have trouble with the first family, *Hundred Chart Hunts*. Underpreparation will lead to what looks like a failed lesson. When you figure out what they don't know— by having watched the students—the process has become an assessment of the class's needs.

When you have identified the missing piece, you have to decide: is this so important that you ought to go back and reteach this concept? Can you do it a different way this time? Or is this actually not as important as you thought? Maybe you should give them a similar but easier problem another day. And maybe you can let it be.

Covering the Material

Problem: You're afraid to do too much group problem solving because it takes so much time. It's good for the students and they like it, but there is material to get through, and at this rate we're not going to make it. This is a tough one.

Some teachers report that they can actually cover *more* material using group activities than without. Group work is good for deep understanding and can be quicker than lecture—and remediation. But there are tradeoffs. You might talk to the person who will teach these students next year and find out what aspects of the students' preparation he or she traditionally gets the most trouble from. Then focus on those.

Some Students Don't Understand

Problem: you're trying to keep everybody involved, but some students are giving up and letting others do all the work. When you look more closely, you see that some students really don't understand what their own clues mean, and therefore can't contribute effectively.

The problems in this book resemble classic jigsaw lessons. Each student brings different information to the group so the whole group can solve its problem. In a way, every student becomes an expert at his or her own clue. Unfortunately, it doesn't always work out quite the way we hope. The jigsaw technique ordinarily requires quite a bit of attention to learning the pieces of information to be brought to the group. In our problems, the students just read their clues. They don't study. And if they don't understand their own clues fully, they're not going to understand the group's solution.

Try giving students some time to think about their clues *before* they start talking. If that doesn't help, put more of the classic jigsaw into the lesson.

Jigsaw

Set up a way for every student to become more familiar with his or her own clue before being thrown into the group setting. Here is one way; use all or part of it:

• Have individual students write about their own clues before solving the problem. The question is: What can you tell about the group's problem (and its solution) based on your one clue?

• Next, students talk with others that have the *same* clue. The same-clue groups discuss what their common clue means and what they know about the solution to the problem. Individual students amend their notes based on this discussion.

• Finally, armed with their original notes, and fortified by the same-clue discussion, the students split up and go back to the regular groups. Since they've explicitly thought about their own clues, they'll be better able to participate.

What can you tell from one clue? For example, if the polygon has no right angles, you know it can't be a square or a rectangle, but it could be a triangle or a rhombus. If Jay and Moira have eleven beans between them, neither of them have twelve. Not all problems work well as jigsaw problems; sometimes individual clues aren't very interesting without the rest. We've included a column in the Topics Grid (page 180) that indicates which families are good for jigsaw. The writing individuals do is a powerful assessment tool. More on that subject on page 112.

Management Note

The easiest way to make this work the first time out is to create your final problem-solving groups first and pass out the clues. Then immediately shuffle the students by bringing the same-clue groups together. You can identify same clues by the blip; see page 12 for a blip diagram. When the students have finished writing alone, discussing, and writing again, have them take their clues and notes back to their original groups to solve the problem.

Another way is to code the problem sets ahead of time—by color or some symbol. Then sort problems into same-clue sets ahead of time, and pass them out to groups. Students write and discuss in the same-clue groups, then go to the problem-solving groups by the code—"all the blues over here; all the goldenrods over there." This scheme has one fewer shuffle of students but requires that you figure the numbers carefully!

School Math

Concept Areas

Logic. Deducing the number of members in a set from information about subsets and supersets. Also, multiple-step problems and plenty of arithmetic.

For Each Group:

- Paper and pencil.

- Manipulatives. Because of large numbers, it might be good to use different types of manipulatives to indicate different quantities (use beans for ones and chips for tens, for example).

Description

Participants have some information about a school, and are asked to deduce more. The number of rooms, the number of periods in a day, the number of teachers, the number of students, and the number of classes each student takes are all interrelated; generally, groups will try to figure out one of these quantities from the others, though there are interesting twists thrown in. For one thing, only one of the four essential clues has the question.

The problems tend to get harder as the population in the problem's school gets older.

Features

Build It, back on page 44, was about logic and spatial reasoning. This family is about logic and numerical reasoning. Consider a problem like, "There were eight M & M's of each color in each of Isabel's bags. Isabel had 25 bags of M & M's, with 2000 M & M's altogether. How many colors of M & M's were there?" There are several things about a problem like that that confuse people:

- it requires multiple steps;

- it uses different operations (multiplication and division); and

- the final question is not the one you expect when you start reading the problem.

The problems in *School Math* occur in a familiar setting—the school—and each has one or more of these attributes. Working the problems in groups will help students overcome the confusion that problems like this sometimes create.

Possible Debriefing Questions

How did you solve the problems?

What did you write down?

What else did you have to figure out on the way?

What else can you tell about the schools where these problems take place?

Were the problems too easy, too hard, or just right? Why?

Echo Echo Elementary

Every classroom in Echo Echo Elementary School has eight tables for students.

Use your information to help your group solve its problem.

Echo Echo Elementary

Every table in a classroom at Echo Echo has four chairs for students.

Here is your group's problem: How many students are there at Echo Echo Elementary School?

Echo Echo Elementary

Echo Echo Elementary is a small school. There are only six classrooms in the whole school.

Drawing a picture might help solve the problem.

Echo Echo Elementary

When every student at Echo Echo Elementary is sitting in a chair at a table, there are still 24 empty chairs in the school.

Use your information to help your group solve its problem.

Echo Echo Elementary

In each classroom, one of the student tables is extra.

Use your information to help your group solve its problem.

Echo Echo Elementary

There are fewer than 175 students at Echo Echo Elementary School.

Here is your group's problem: How many students are there at Echo Echo Elementary School?

from *Get It Together* • EQUALS, Lawrence Hall of Science

King Middle School

King Middle School has 1200 students.

Be sure your group knows what the problem is before it tries to solve it!

King Middle School

Each student at King takes six classes a day.

Use your clue to help the group solve the problem.

King Middle School

Each class at King has thirty students and one teacher.

Use your clue to help your group solve its problem.

King Middle School

Every teacher at King teaches five classes a day (They each have one free period for planning).

Here's the problem: How many teachers are there at King Middle School?

King Middle School

There are forty classes going on each period at King Middle School.

How many teachers are there at King Middle School?

King Middle School

Every student at King has to take a class during each of the six periods.

Lunch doesn't count as a period for anybody.

 from *Get It Together* • EQUALS, Lawrence Hall of Science

Harthan Homeroom

The thirty classrooms at Harthan Junior High are filled every period except homeroom.

How many students are there in each homeroom?

Harthan Homeroom

Three of the classrooms are not used as homerooms, but there are the same number of students in each homeroom.

How many students are there in each homeroom?

Harthan Homeroom

There are thirty students in every class (except PE and homeroom) at Harthan J.H.S.

How many students are there in each homeroom?

Harthan Homeroom

One-sixth of the students are in PE every period—except homeroom, when all students are in their homerooms.

How many students are there in each homeroom?

Harthan Homeroom

Nine of the classroom teachers have no homeroom.

How many students are there in each homeroom?

Harthan Homeroom

There are thirty-six classroom teachers at Harthan Junior High, each of whom teach five periods.

How many students are there in each homeroom?

from *Get It Together* • EQUALS, Lawrence Hall of Science

Field Trip

There's a rule at Inigo Montoya Middle School that says that you can't split up a class when you load it onto a school bus.

When the entire seventh grade went on a field trip, how many buses did it take?

Field Trip

On the day of the field trip, no seventh grade class had more than 35 students or fewer than twenty. They loaded into StratoMaster deLuxe School Buses (the ones with the working windows), each of which can seat fifty students.

Ignore the teachers in this problem. They go by car. (Remember: this is fiction.)

Field Trip

On the day of the field trip, all of the classes at Inigo Montoya Middle School had different numbers of students. And none of the seventh-grade teachers could divide their classes evenly into teams of three or five.

Field Trip

Montoya Middle has lots of rules. One says that you have to start loading buses with the largest class waiting to load. If the next class won't fit, the bus leaves and you start a new bus.

When all eight classrooms of the seventh grade at Inigo Montoya Middle School went on a field trip, how many buses did it take?

Field Trip

If the rules allowed classes to be mixed when loading buses, they could've taken care of the field trip with five busloads. Unfortunately, everybody followed the rules.

How many buses did it take when they followed the rules?

Field Trip

The seventh grade at Inigo Montoya Middle School was going on a field trip to a llama ranch. The second-to-last bus to be loaded had 49 students in it. That was the fullest bus that day.

How many buses did it take altogether to take the seventh grade on this field trip?

Heddupp High

During each of the six periods, exactly one-sixth of the students at Heddupp High take PE.

Everybody goes to lunch at the same time.

Use your clues to help your group solve the problem.

Heddupp High

The *average* non-PE class size at Helen Heddupp High (HHH) is thirty students.

There is a short recess between second and third period.

How many students take PE first period at HHH?

Heddupp High

Eighteen of the twenty-four classroom teachers at Heddupp High teach five non-PE classes and have one prep period.

Lunch is between fourth and fifth period.

How many students take PE first period at Helen Heddupp High?

Heddupp High

The cafeteria at Heddupp High is famous for a dessert the students call "Apple Death."

Six of the classroom teachers at Heddupp High have only three regular classes a day.

How many students take PE first period at Helen Heddupp High?

Heddupp High

There are more than 630 students at Helen Heddupp High.

This rural high school was named for Helen Heddupp, who once owned much of the Anderson Valley, famous for its apples.

How many students take PE first period at Heddupp High?

Heddupp High

There are twenty-one classrooms at Heddupp High, but during any period, three of them are empty.

Use your clues to help your group solve the problem.

Venn Family

Concept Areas

Logic of sets and subsets. Set membership and attributes. Logical words such as BOTH, AND, and NOT. Venn diagrams.

For Each Group:

- Manipulatives.

- Venn circles.

Circles made of string or yarn are good, but we found that circles drawn on scratch paper don't twist and get separated. You can make the problems easier by providing (unlabeled) Venn diagrams with the appropriate number of circles.

Description

Individual clues tell you something about the objects being discussed, for example, "Some swimmers are also divers," or "1/4 of all the birds are swans." The group has to figure out how many objects are in every possible region on the Venn diagram representing the sets in the problem, though the actual questions the group must answer are more like, "how many swimmers are there altogether?" These questions may be distributed among the group members' clues.

Other Comments

Manipulatives and group work will help give all students some success experience in the confusing world of sets and set membership. While it is not essential, these problems are most appropriate for a group that has been exposed to Venn diagrams.

But do you *have* to use Venn diagrams? Of course not! We have seen some wonderful solutions to similar problems from students who had never heard of Venn diagrams. They invented their own ways to organize the information, and came to solid solutions.

Possible Debriefing Questions

How different were the diagrams the groups created?

Is there a better way to solve these problems? Can you think of another kind of diagram?

Do all Venn diagrams have to be circles? Can you make other shapes to represent the sets?

Why are they called Venn diagrams?

Can you think of a problem where Venn diagrams won't help?

Swimmers and Divers

Some Swimers are also Divers.

Some Divers are also Swimmers.

How many Swimmers are there?
How many Divers?

Swimmers and Divers

There are a total of twelve
Swimmers and Divers.

How many Swimmers are there?
How many Divers?

Swimmers and Divers

Two Swimmers are also Divers.

How many Swimmers are there?
How many Divers?

Swimmers and Divers

Four Divers are not Swimmers

How many Swimmers are there?
How many Divers?

Swimmers and Divers

1/3 of all the Divers
are also Swimmers.

How many Swimmers are there?
How many Divers?

Swimmers and Divers

1/4 of all the Swimmers
are also Divers.

How many Swimmers are there?
How many Divers?

Swimmers

Divers

© 1989 The Regents of the University of California

from *Get It Together* • EQUALS, Lawrence Hall of Science

Fowl Pets

Some ducks are also pets, and some pets are also geese—but no ducks are geese.

There are three different questions your group has to answer! It might help to draw a Venn diagram.

Fowl Pets

Four of the ducks are not pets.
One pet is neither a duck nor a goose.

How many ducks are there?

Fowl Pets

Only one of the pets is a goose.

There are a total of ten birds. How many of them are pets?

Fowl Pets

Two geese are not pets.

How many geese are there?

Fowl Pets

Half of all the pets are ducks.

Your group has three questions to answer. Use your clue to help the group.

Fowl Pets

Eight of the birds are either ducks or pets (or both).

Your group has three questions to answer. Use your clue to help the group.

Ducks

Pets

Geese

from *Get It Together* • EQUALS, Lawrence Hall of Science

Tiffs, Riffs, and Pix

Some Tiffs are also Riffs and Pix.
Some Riffs are also Tiffs and Pix.
Some Pix are also Tiffs and Riffs.

There are three different questions
your group has to answer!

Tiffs, Riffs, and Pix

Three Tiffs are not Riffs or Pix.
Five Riffs are not Tiffs or Pix.
Six Pix are not Tiffs or Riffs.

How many Riffs are there?

Tiffs, Riffs, and Pix

Two Tiffs are also Pix but not Riffs.
One Riff is also a Tiff but not a Pix.
Four Pix are also Riffs but not Tiffs.

How many Tiffs are there?

Tiffs, Riffs, and Pix

Two Tiffs are also Pix and Riffs at the
same time.

How many Pix are there altogether?

Tiffs, Riffs, and Pix

The are a total of nine Tiffs
and Riffs that are not Pix.

Your group has three questions to
answer. Use your clue to help the
group.

Tiffs, Riffs, and Pix

There are a total of 23 Tiffs, Riffs and
Pix.

Your group has three questions to
answer. Use your clue to help the
group.

Tiffs

Riffs

Pix

© 1989 The Regents of the University of California

from *Get It Together* • EQUALS, Lawrence Hall of Science

Grups, Dwarts, & Teasles

Every Grup is a Dwart.
No Teasle is a Grup.

How many Dwarts are neither
Grups nor Teasles?

Grups, Dwarts, & Teasles

Half of all Teasles are also Dwarts.

How many Dwarts are neither
Grups nor Teasles?

Grups, Dwarts, & Teasles

There are 30 Teasles, but only 20
Grups.

How many Dwarts are neither
Grups nor Teasles?

Grups, Dwarts, & Teasles

Half of all Dwarts are also Grups.

How many Dwarts are neither
Grups nor Teasles?

Grups, Dwarts, & Teasles

Some Dwarts are only Dwarts, and
some Teasles are only Teasles, but
no Grups are only Grups.

How many Dwarts are neither
Grups nor Teasles?

Grups, Dwarts, & Teasles

There are 25 Dwarts that are not
Teasles.

How many Dwarts are neither
Grups nor Teasles?

Grups
Dwarts
Teasles

from Get It Together • EQUALS, Lawrence Hall of Science

Breakfast, Anyone?

Only one student had *everything* that was offered for breakfast. She had juice, cereal and eggs.

How many students had something for breakfast?

Breakfast, Anyone?

Nine students had juice for breakfast, but only two had nothing else.

How many students had something for breakfast?

Breakfast, Anyone?

The same number of students had juice and cereal (without eggs) as had cereal by itself.

How many students had something for breakfast?

Breakfast, Anyone?

Five students had eggs, but only one had them without anything else. Eight students had no eggs at all.

How many students had something for breakfast?

Breakfast, Anyone?

Four students had juice and eggs for breakfast.

How many students had something for breakfast?

Breakfast, Anyone?

No one had eggs and cereal without juice.

How many students had something for breakfast?

Eggs

Cereal

Juice

from *Get It Together* • EQUALS, Lawrence Hall of Science

Lineup Logic

Concept Areas

Logic and spatial reasoning.
Finding alternative solutions and
the process of elimination. Creating
problem-solving strategies.

For Each Group:

- Labels that you will cut from each sheet of
  clues. Include them in the problem
  envelopes.

- Manipulatives.

- Pencil and paper.

Description

Each problem in this family requires the group to
put something in order based on the clues.
People in the problem are playing dodgeball, or
lining up for a photo session, or something, and
the clues help us figure out who is next to whom.
"Mai couldn't stand next to her best friend."
"Imogen was directly across from Aloysius."

This type of logic problem is different from the
typical puzzle-book variety where you draw a
chart and use the process of elimination. It's
harder to be systematic here, so students are
more likely to have to develop problem-solving
strategies anew rather than apply some canned
procedure.

Still, doing a few of these helps students develop
effective techniques: start with a part of the order
that you know. Try possible solutions. Review
what you have. Adjust. Ensure that the parts that
you have secure don't get disturbed as you move
things around.

Debriefing Suggestion

These problems are excellent
examples of problems in which
some groups will notice that the
order of clues matters. It is
therefore a good problem family
in which to discuss this in
debriefing and to have students
suggest ways to deal with this
problem. Letting everybody read
their clues first and then decide
where to start is one effective
solution; what others will your
students find?

Photo Lineup

Keisha is almost the tallest. Otis is almost the shortest.

José was disappointed that he couldn't stand next to John.

Who is standing next to whom?

Photo Lineup

Kevin has three kids on each side of him in the picture.

Who is standing next to whom?

Photo Lineup

John and Luanne are standing on the ends.

José and Angela are not next to each other.

Who is standing next to whom?

Photo Lineup

Otis is the only boy that is standing between two girls.

Angela didn't get to stand next to her best friend.

Who is standing next to whom?

Photo Lineup

The students are lined up from tallest to shortest.

Who is standing next to whom?

Photo Lineup

There are 7 students in this photo line-up.

Angela and Luanne are best friends.

Who is standing next to whom?

Keisha   Kevin   Otis   José   Luanne   Angela   John

from *Get It Together* • EQUALS, Lawrence Hall of Science

Dodgeball

Franz is on Mai's right and John and Mohammed are the only boys standing next to a boy.

Who is standing next to whom?

Dodgeball

Eight friends are standing in a circle playing dodgeball. Mai is standing between two boys, but Kate is on Alisa's left.

Who is standing next to whom?

Dodgeball

There are three people standing between Janice and Mohammed.

Who is standing next to whom?

Dodgeball

Lincoln is standing directly across from John, but Janice is just clockwise from Lincoln.

Who is standing next to whom?

Dodgeball

There are eight kids playing dodgeball.

Who is standing next to whom?

Dodgeball

In this problem, all of the children whose names end in a vowel are girls.

Who is standing next to whom?

Franz   John   Mai   Alisa   Kate   Mohammed   Janice   Lincoln

from Get It Together • EQUALS, Lawrence Hall of Science

Police Line Up!

The ten suspects were lined up by height.

Babs is taller than Nance.

Red is taller than Ted.

Jack is shorter than Vic.

Police Line Up!

Red is shorter than Nance.

Sal is shorter than Mo.

Babs is taller than Todd.

Who ate the pecan pie?

Police Line Up!

Al is taller than Red.

Todd is taller than Mo.

Nance is shorter than Sal.

Two people ate the pecan pie.

Police Line Up!

Al is shorter than Nance.

Babs is taller than Vic.

Mo is shorter than Jack.

The two in the middle are guilty!

Police Line Up!

Babs is taller than Ted.

Vic is taller than Red.

Sal is shorter than Jack.

Police Line Up!

Al is shorter than Mo.

Nance is shorter than Todd.

Babs is taller than Al.

Jack | Sal | Ted | Babs | Red | Nance | Vic | Mo | Todd | Al

from *Get It Together* • EQUALS, Lawrence Hall of Science

Interstate 99

Albany and Flint are the closest cities to each other; Albany is just one mile south of Flint.

Order the cities North to South.

Interstate 99

Leaving Flint, you pass next through Furndale on your way to Seaview.

All six of the cities are on Interstate 99.

Interstate 99

The city of Ridgemont is north of Albany and the city of Compton is south.

Interstate 99 is a big highway that runs from North to South.

Interstate 99

The city of Seaview is on Lake Michigan and this is where Interstate #99 ends.

Order the cities North to South.

Interstate 99

There are six cities along this stretch of Interstate #99.

Order the cities North to South.

Interstate 99

Seaview and Compton are the furthest apart.

Order the cities North to South.

Albany

Flint

Furndale

Seaview

Ridgemont

Compton

© 1989 The Regents of the University of California

from *Get It Together* • EQUALS, Lawrence Hall of Science

Who's With Horace?

Eight friends came to the party, two at a time, but no one arrived with someone whose name rhymes with their own.

Who's With Horace?

Fern arrived after both Vern and Doris.

Who came with Horace?

Who's With Horace?

Zoe and Chloe both arrived before Horace. Who did Horace arrive with?

Who's With Horace?

Pearl and Merle both arrived before Zoe and Vern.

Who came with Horace?

Who's With Horace?

Doris arrived with Pearl.

But who arrived with Horace?

Who's With Horace?

Zoe and Vern arrived together.

Who arrived with Horace?

Horace   Doris   Fern   Vern   Zoe   Chloe   Merle   Pearl

from *Get It Together* • EQUALS, Lawrence Hall of Science

Mysteries

Concept Areas

Logic. The process of elimination, cause and effect, truth and falsehood. Also, proof by contradiction.

Other Comments

Mystery problems are engaging and exciting. Unfortunately, too many of them involve people getting murdered. While murder may be a riveting element in novel and drama plots, we think our students get enough of it on TV. So we have tried to come up with mystery problems in which no crime is committed, though people do get sick.

We believe that this is an equity issue. Many people are uninterested in death by foul play; we shouldn't tie their mathematics education to it!

For Each Group:

* Labels that you will cut from each sheet of clues. Include them in the problem envelopes.

* Paper and pencil.

Description

These are logic problems in which we have to figure out something based on indirect information. In the problem, "What Went Bad?" for example, we learn who ate what at a potluck and who got sick. We have to figure out which food was the culprit. These problems vary in their themes and the logic you have to use to solve them.

Students can become adept at solving some traditional cooperative logic problems—ones that use the process of elimination and can be solved with a grid—while losing sight of the underlying reasoning. These mystery problems break out of that set. Reasoning about cause and effect adds another dimension to the logic, as does wondering whether the clues are true or not (See *Samantha's Second Surprise*). *Mantissa's Memory* is really about controlling variables, and one problem—*Dorm Disease*—also presents students with the problem of having to manage a great deal of information.

Suggested Debriefing Questions

How did you use the manipulatives?

What problem-solving strategies did you use?

Are there any other solutions to these problems? If not, how do you know?

(In *Mantissa's Memory*) What would you do in order to make a 36-foot-long dragon?

Can you think up other mystery problems in which no one gets hurt?

Mantissa's Memory

Mantissa is trying to remember the formula for the potion that will turn her into a 72-foot-long dragon.

When she tried three eagle feathers, salamander breath, and scales from a rainbow trout, she only turned into a six-foot-long dragon. She barely burnt her toast.

Mantissa's Memory

Mantissa remembers that the potion needs three feathers from either a penguin or an eagle. But she can't remember which.

When she tried penguin feathers, salamander breath, and scales from a rainbow trout, she turned into a twelve-foot-long dragon. Not bad, but not enough.

Mantissa's Memory

Mantissa remembers that the potion calls for some breath — from a salamander. Or is it a frog?

She tried the frog's breath with three penguin feathers and scales from a rainbow trout. The resulting dragon was only 24 feet long. What's the recipe for a 72-foot dragon?

Mantissa's Memory

Mantissa remembers that the scales in the potion are either from a fence lizard or a rainbow trout.

When she drank a potion made from fence lizard scales, three eagle feathers, and the breath of a salamander, she changed into a dragon that was eighteen feet long and set her couch on fire.

Mantissa's Memory

The active ingredients in a potion to change you into a dragon are some scales, three feathers, and some breath, but Mantissa can't remember which is from what.

She *does* remember, though, that picking the right scales makes the biggest difference.

Mantissa's Memory

Seventy-two feet is the longest dragon you can make with this recipe. And that's the one you have to help Mantissa remember.

Variations on the recipe make only smaller dragons. For example, eagle feathers, frog breath, and rainbow trout scales make a dragon only twelve feet long.

from *Get It Together* • EQUALS, Lawrence Hall of Science

What Went Bad?

Beatrice got sick after the pot-luck.

Jason ate desert chicken, but not swamp chicken.

Everyone who ate the food that went bad got sick. What was it?

What Went Bad?

Camilla and Jason both had cheesecake.

Alfie ate everything except the pineapple upside-down cake and the desert chicken.

Only one of the five foods was bad.

What Went Bad?

Alfie, Beatrice, Camilla, and Jason attended a school pot-luck together. The next day two of them were sick. Which food went bad?

Alfie was one of the friends who did not get sick.

What Went Bad?

Camilla was the only one who didn't eat the baked beans.

Jason felt fine the day after the dinner.

What Went Bad?

Two of the four friends ate swamp chicken.

The five dishes at the (rather small) pot-luck dinner were swamp chicken, desert chicken, baked beans, pineapple upside-down cake, and cheesecake.

What Went Bad?

All of the friends ate three dishes except Beatrice, who ate four.

Camilla ate two desserts.

Only three of the four friends ate cheesecake.

Dorm Disease

Only Sherry and Perry were still well at the end of the day.

Barry met Jerri at 1 pm while Teri met Perry. Harry met Jerri at 10 am. Barry, Carrie, and Gary spoke at four in the afternoon.

Who was sick first?

Dorm Disease

Only one person was sick before nine AM, but anyone who spoke with a sick person got sick instantly.

Mary, Larry, and Gary met briefly at ten. At two, Jerri met Teri, Sherry met Carrie, and Mary met Gary.

Who was sick first?

Dorm Disease

This whole problem takes place between 9 AM and 4 PM on the same day in Aaron Airy Dorm.

Carrie, Teri, and Mary had breakfast together at nine. Jerri met Sherry for lunch at twelve; they saw Larry and Mary sitting together at another table. Who was sick first?

Dorm Disease

The sick people kept walking around and talking to others—they didn't know they were really sick 'til dinner.

Barry, Mary and Harry met at eleven, the same time that Gary and Teri met. Carrie and Teri met twice: once at ten and once at three. Who was sick first?

Dorm Disease

Oddly enough, Perry never spoke to Sherry the whole day. Harry and Larry didn't meet until four.

Who got sick first?

Dorm Disease

Everyone in Aaron Airy Dorm was meeting in small groups to plan the InterDorm Dance. Mary met with Harry at three.

Perry, Gary, and Teri all had lunch together at twelve.

Who got sick first?

 from Get It Together • EQUALS, Lawrence Hall of Science

Samantha's Surprise

When Samantha asked Ophelia, Ophelia replied, "I'm not going to tell you, but we'd have been better organized if one person told everybody. As it was, no one told more than one other person."

Your group's task is to figure out who *organized* Samantha's party.

Samantha's Surprise

When Samantha asked Quentin who organized the party, he said, "I won't tell you who organized it, but I will tell you that Penelope found out from Rupert."

The person who organized the party is not the one who thought up the idea.

Samantha's Surprise

Rupert told Samantha: "I won't tell you who organized the party, but that person did find out about the party from the person who thought up the idea in the first place."

Samantha's Surprise

Samantha asked Penelope who organized the party. Penelope said, "I wish I had thought up the idea, but I was the last to hear. Quentin didn't think of it either."

Samantha's Surprise

Samantha's friends gave her a surprise party. She had such a good time, she asked them questions to find out who organized it. Though they all told her the truth, they tried to be evasive. Still, she figured it out. Can your group?

Use your clues to help your group—you may read your clue but you may not show it to anyone.

Penelope

Quentin

Rupert

Ophelia

from *Get It Together* • EQUALS, Lawrence Hall of Science

Samantha's Second Surprise

When Samantha asked Ophelia, Ophelia replied, "Penelope organized the party this year."

Your group's task is to figure out who organized Samantha's party.

Samantha's Second Surprise

When Samantha asked Quentin who organized the party, he said, "I won't tell you who organized it, but I didn't do it."

Your group's task is to figure out who organized Samantha's party.

Samantha's Second Surprise

When Samantha asked Rupert who organized the party, he told her that Penelope did it.

Who organized the party? Use your clue to help the group figure it out.

Samantha's Second Surprise

Samantha asked Penelope who organized the party. Penelope said, "Okay, I'll tell you: Ophelia did it."

Who organized the party? Use your clue to help the group figure it out.

Samantha's Second Surprise

Samantha's friends gave her a surprise party again! Once again, she asked them questions to find out who organized it. This time, only one of her four friends told the truth; the other three lied. Still, she figured it out. Can your group?

Use your clues to help your group—you may read your clue but you may not show it to anyone.

Penelope	Quentin	Rupert	Ophelia
Truth	Lie	Lie	Lie

from *Get It Together* • EQUALS, Lawrence Hall of Science

Which Spinner

Concept Areas

Probability and properties of spinners. The concept, "equally likely." Combining numbers and the likelihood of combinations.

For Each Group:

- The drawing of sixteen spinners labelled A through R from the facing page. Each of the first two problems only use half the mat: A through H or J through R.

- Manipulatives to mark the mat.

Description

The solution to each problem is one of the spinners on the mat. Individual clues eliminate one or more of the spinners on the mat; whichever one is left is the spinner. Clues might be simple, like "There are four different numbers on this spinner" to clues that use more of a knowledge of probability, such as, "it is impossible to get a sum of five in two spins with this spinner."

Learning About Probability

Never ever do a problem in this family or the next until your students have experience spinning genuine spinners.

Students need to spin spinners and predict what will happen. They need to make graphs of their results. They need to make spinners of their own. Only then can they start on the abstract road to which problems like these are a gateway.

Other Comments

This family—*Which Spinner*—comes before *Draw the Spinner*, which begins on page 106, because recognizing something ought to be easier than producing it. Yet in the first field test, students did much better on those problems—*Draw the Spinner*—than on these supposedly easier ones. It turned out that the probability content in the two families was not the problem. Instead, the students didn't know how to eliminate possibilities—or even recognize the process of elimination as an appropriate logical technique.

Thus, using these *Which Spinner* problems became an assessment tool: we discovered that the students didn't have a problem-solving strategy we thought they had. We concentrated on learning about the process of elimination in a variety of settings (there are plenty in this book). We could do that in a manner complementary to the instruction about spinners and probability.

Possible Debriefing Questions

How did you decide on the answer?

Were any clues more important than any others?

Have you played any games that use spinners?

What other ways do you know of producing a random result?

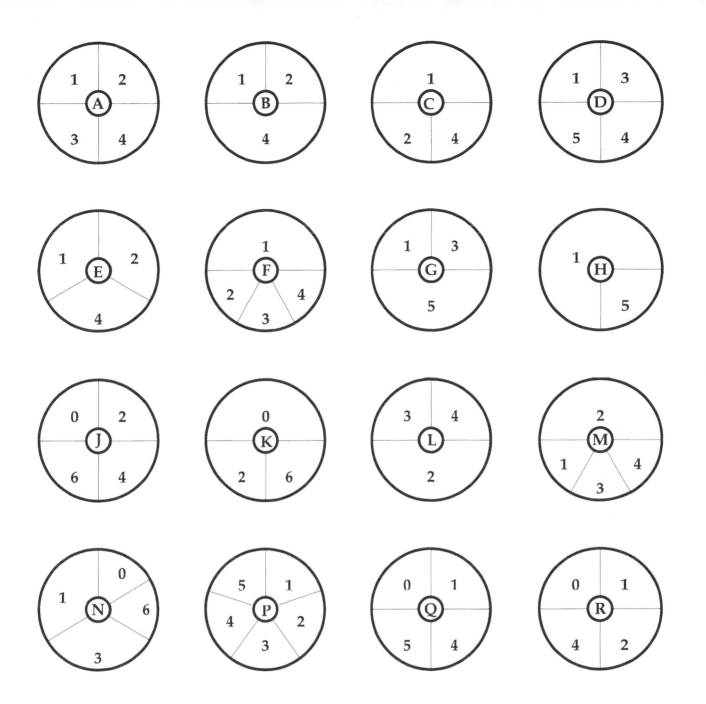

Spinner Sheet

from *Get It Together* • EQUALS, Lawrence Hall of Science

A–H Spinners!

A–H Spinners!

A–H Spinners!

A–H Spinners!

A–H Spinners!

A–H Spinners!

from *Get It Together* • EQUALS, Lawrence Hall of Science

Spinners JR

You can't make a sum of ten in two spins with this spinner, but you can do it in three.

The spinner is one of the spinners between J and R on the spinner sheet. Use your clue to help the group figure out which one!

Spinners JR

It's possible to get a one when you spin this spinner.

The spinner is one of the spinners between J and R on the spinner sheet. Use your clue to help the group figure out which one!

Spinners JR

There is less than a 50% chance that you will spin a two in one spin.

The spinner is one of the spinners between J and R on the spinner sheet. Use your clue to help the group figure out which one!

Spinners JR

The numbers on the spinner are *not* equally likely to show up.

The spinner is one of the spinners between J and R on the spinner sheet. Use your clue to help the group figure out which one!

Spinners JR

It's possible that after 100 spins, the sum of all your spins will still be zero.

The spinner is one of the spinners between J and R on the spinner sheet. Use your clue to help the group figure out which one!

Spinners JR

If you spin this spinner twice, the numbers will sometimes add up to two.

The spinner is one of the spinners between J and R on the spinner sheet. Use your clue to help the group figure out which one!

Which Spinner #1

It's impossible to spin a two in one spin with this spinner.

Which spinner is it?

The spinner is one of the spinners on the spinner sheet. Use your clue to help the group figure out which one!

Which Spinner #1

You'll never get a six with this spinner in one spin no matter how long you try.

The spinner is one of the spinners on the spinner sheet. Use your clue to help the group figure out which one!

Which Spinner #1

The chance of spinning a five is not the same as the chance of spinning a one.

The spinner is one of the spinners on the spinner sheet. Use your clue to help the group figure out which one!

Which Spinner #1

If you spun this spinner 100 times you'd probably get only twenty or thirty fives.

The spinner is one of the spinners on the spinner sheet. Use your clue to help the group figure out which one!

Which Spinner #1

If you spun this spinner 100 times and added up all the numbers, you'd probably get about 200.

The spinner is one of the spinners on the spinner sheet. Use your clue to help the group figure out which one!

Which Spinner #1

If you spun this spinner twice and added, you'd never get a five.

The spinner is one of the spinners on the spinner sheet. Use your clue to help the group figure out which one!

from *Get It Together* • EQUALS, Lawrence Hall of Science

Which Spinner #2

It is not possible to spin a sum of seven in two spins with this spinner.

The spinner is one of the spinners on the spinner sheet. Use your clue to help the group figure out which one!

Which Spinner #2

It is possible to get a ten with this spinner in two spins if you add the numbers.

The spinner is one of the spinners on the spinner sheet. Use your clue to help the group figure out which one!

Which Spinner #2

The chance of a spinner landing on a three in two spins with this spinner is zero. No chance at all.

The spinner is one of the spinners on the spinner sheet. Use your clue to help the group figure out which one!

Which Spinner #2

There are more ways to get a sum of five in two spins than a sum of one in two spins.

The spinner is one of the spinners on the spinner sheet. Use your clue to help the group figure out which one!

Which Spinner #2

In a hundred spins, the sum of the numbers you'll get is about the same as for spinner A.

The spinner is one of the spinners on the spinner sheet. Use your clue to help the group figure out which one!

Which Spinner #2

There are four numbers on this spinner.

Which spinner is it?

The spinner is one of the spinners on the spinner sheet. Use your clue to help the group figure out which one!

from *Get It Together* • EQUALS, Lawrence Hall of Science

Draw the Spinner

Concept Areas

Probability. Likelihood of independent events related to spinners, averages, the law of large numbers, combinations of numbers, the probabilities of certain sums.

For Each Group:

- Paper and pencil.

Description

In contrast to the *Which Spinner* family, in which students had to find the spinner on the sheet that fits the clues, in this family, students have to draw the spinner, not just recognize it.

In addition, the last problems in this set are more subtle, throwing problem-solvers a variety of curves, such as negative numbers and fractions.

Be sure to read about learning probability on page 100.

Other Comments

Many of us believe that education in probability and statistics is a sex equity issue. Boy games are frequently obsessed with statistics and with probabilistic results. Dolls never roll dice. Does that matter? You bet. Understanding statistics and probability are important for success in math-based fields—and traditional math textbooks pay no more than a few pages' attention to it. So if we want to teach statistics and probability to benefit our students' mathematical futures, we will need materials and activities to supplement textbooks at all levels.

And needing to know about probability and statistics isn't limited to those who want math-based careers. As citizens, we're bombarded with statistics all the time; we need to learn to make sense of them. While these problems do not make up a course in statistical literacy, they form part of what every student should have: a broad experiential base in simple probability.

Possible Debriefing Questions

Have you played any games that use spinners?

Could you make a spinner that replaces the dice in *Monopoly*?

Could you make a spinner to model the weather? What labels would you put on the different sections?

Draw the spinner 1

There are three numbers on the spinner. Four is the largest number.

Draw the spinner!

Draw the spinner 1

One of the numbers on the spinner comes up about half of the time.

Draw the spinner!

Draw the spinner 1

The number "two" comes up about a quarter of the time.

Draw the spinner!

Draw the spinner 1

The most likely number to come up on this spinner is 1 (one).

Draw the spinner!

Draw the spinner 1

If you add the three numbers on the spinner, you get seven.

Draw the spinner!

Draw the spinner 1

If you spin the spinner twice and add the numbers, it's possible to get eight but never seven.

Draw the spinner!

from *Get It Together* • EQUALS, Lawrence Hall of Science

Draw the spinner 2

The four numbers on the spinner are equally likely. They are also all different.

Draw the spinner!

Draw the spinner 2

It's impossible to get an odd number if you spin this spinner twice and add the results.

Draw the spinner!

Draw the spinner 2

The most likely sum of two spins of this spinner is eight.

Draw the spinner!

Draw the spinner 2

The smallest sum you can get in two spins of this spinner is 2; the largest is 14.

Draw the spinner!

Draw the spinner 2

It's impossible to get an even number on this spinner if you spin three times and add.

Draw the spinner!

Draw the spinner 2

If you spin this spinner twice, and add the two numbers, you're just as likely to get 10 as 6.

Draw the spinner!

from *Get It Together* • EQUALS, Lawrence Hall of Science

Draw the spinner 3

There are three different numbers on the spinner, all integers — but one of them is less than zero.

Draw the spinner!

Draw the spinner 3

Two of the numbers on the spinner are equally likely; the other comes up about half the time.

Draw the spinner!

Draw the spinner 3

The largest number you can get on two spins of this spinner is six.

Draw the spinner!

Draw the spinner 3

Though you'll never get zero in one spin, the *average* spin on this spinner is zero.

Draw the spinner!

Draw the spinner 3

You can't make zero on two spins with this spinner, but you can do it in three.

Draw the spinner!

Draw the spinner 3

If you add all three numbers on the spinner, you get 2.

Draw the spinner!

from *Get It Together* • EQUALS, Lawrence Hall of Science

Draw the spinner 4

The three numbers on the spinner are equally likely, and no two are the same.

Draw the spinner!

Draw the spinner 4

Five times out of nine, the spinner below will show a higher number than the spinner you're supposed to draw—and there are no ties.

Draw the spinner!

Draw the spinner 4

All of the numbers on the spinner are positive integers, and all are single digits.

Draw the spinner!

Draw the spinner 4

If you spin this spinner twice and add, you'll always get an even number.

Draw the spinner!

Draw the spinner 4

The smallest number you can get if you sum two spins of this spinner is four.

Draw the spinner!

Draw the spinner 4

The most likely number you'll get if you sum six spins of this spinner is 32.

Draw the spinner!

from *Get It Together* • EQUALS, Lawrence Hall of Science

Draw the spinner 5

The spinner has three sections. While no two are the same size, one of the sections is half the size of another.

Draw the spinner!

Draw the spinner 5

The largest number you can get in two spins of this spinner is one.

Draw the spinner!

Draw the spinner 5

If you spin the spinner twice and add, you get a sum of one about a quarter of the time.

Draw the spinner!

Draw the spinner 5

You're more likely to get 2/3 than one if you sum two spins, but 5/6 is the most likely sum of all.

Draw the spinner!

Draw the spinner 5

If you spun the spinner a hundred times and added up all the numbers, you'd probably get somewhere near 40.

Draw the spinner!

Draw the spinner 5

The sum of the three numbers on the spinner is one.

Draw the spinner!

from *Get It Together* • EQUALS, Lawrence Hall of Science

Assessment

It's hard to break out of the mold that says assessment is a test and that assessment comes at the end. We should try to assess our students continuously, if possible. Even in the case of summative assessment—what you *do* do at the end to find out what happened—the process of assessment begins before the beginning, when you plan what to assess and how that's going to happen. All too often, we assess out of habit—we give a test on the content—rather than out of planning. Don't believe for a minute that *assessment* and *grading* are the same thing. Furthermore, we need to remember that we need to assess both the students and the lesson.

Assessing Students and Groups

You might want to use a test or a worksheet that the students will complete individually. You can also consult some of the resources (page 177) for strategies for group testing. But traditional tests are not really very informative. Here we will stress some alternative strategies because we can see so much richness in what the students do in groups.

Informal Observation

The first thing to do is to watch—and watch something specific, perhaps one academic or one social behavior. Don't try to watch too many things! You might pick "persistence." Before you watch, try to imagine how you would tell if a student were persisting or not. What behaviors do you expect to see? She will probably be listening to what the group has to say, working actively on the problem, and not looking around the room. You may even want to tell the class that those are the things you will be looking for. Students can learn to assess themselves by becoming conscious of their actions.

Take notes on what you see, trying to focus on the aspects of the lesson you decided on ahead of time, but noting other interesting or revealing occurrences.

Formal observation

You can be more formal about it by tallying occurrences of what you see next to a class list, or listing initials next to behaviors. This has several advantages: first, you can make sure you know whom you've observed. Depending on what you're looking for, you may not be able to observe everyone adequately. If you don't get around, you'll know whom to concentrate on tomorrow. Second, you'll have a quantitative measure that you can use to help you analyze what's going on in your class and that will increase your legitimacy in the eyes of people who rely on quantitative measures.

There are disadvantages, however, in that you are quantifying something that may be hard—or dangerous—to quantify. It would be ridiculous—if Samuel got a 6 in persistence when Letitia scored an 8—to label Sam a dilettante.

Keep your eyes open. Reserve a space on that clipboard for other notes, for recording the juicy things that you will always see in a group activity, things that will appear in this session's debriefing or on next week's observation sheet.

Papers from the Session

During the course of a group problem-solving session, groups will write down attempts at solutions and final products. You can collect these and evaluate them in order to see what individuals and the class know.

These papers might be normal scratch paper. For example, with the *Constructions* family, students will make geometrical drawings; these drawings themselves are rich windows into the thinking of the group members. It's easy to tell who is off track and who is on.

You might also structure the session so that students write particular things at particular times, especially if you're using a jigsaw format (see page 75).

Writing

Writing is a powerful educational tool and a rich source of information about students' thinking. Benefits that come from "talking math" accrue to writers about mathematics: deeper understanding of concepts and processes, more organized thinking, another mode of learning, as well as improved writing skills and a better appreciation for connectedness in education.

But writing for assessment? Sure! If you ask students to write what they know about polygons, for example, you will get written work that can form part of an assessment package. Keep the papers (or copies of them) and create a portfolio for each student that you can refer to as you make inevitable grading decisions—something beyond an array of test scores. A writing portfolio reflects the quality of a student's thinking and the tangible progress he or she has made.

Most students are not used to writing about mathematics, so you may be disappointed at first. Don't despair! With your constructive comments, the discussion of their peers, and with practice, every student's writing will improve. Hold a class meeting on how to make important ideas stand out; be sure to have students read and comment on one another's writing.

What to write is another question. Writing can be about process or content; it can be long or short, polished or rough. You may want to start with a few words (five words that have to do with polygons) or a list (everything you know about polygons). Maybe the groups can brainstorm the list and the individuals can write the paragraphs with complete sentences. They might write about the mathematics or about *how* the group solved the problem.

But you don't have to read all that writing! Don't feel you have to read each paper thoroughly. Take a fine comb to a sample, and glance at the rest. You'll be amazed at how much you'll learn—it's like being inside their heads!

Assessing Yourself and the Lesson

You need to take time—it doesn't have to be much—to reflect for yourself on how a cooperative lesson went. In the heat of the moment, it's hard to keep your finger on everything that happens. It's important to separate behavior from interpretation and actual occurrences from impressions. So, as soon as possible after the lesson, take time to answer for yourself questions like these:

- For which students do I have a clear idea of what they did in the lesson and what they know afterwards?

- Are there any students whom I can't remember even being in the class?

- Did I adhere to the norms of behavior? Did I intervene unnecessarily?

- Was I well-enough prepared for the lesson? Too-well prepared?

- Did I ask some Really Good questions that helped students figure things out for themselves? Better still, did I hear a student ask such a question?

- Did I allow enough time for debriefing?

- Did anything that happened surprise me?

Build it Again

Concept Areas

Geometry and spatial reasoning in three dimensions, logic in a geometrical setting. Using vocabulary: cube, face, edge, side, center, rectangle, touching, above, below, each, every.

For Each Group:

- Colored cubes. More cubes than in *Build It*, including purples.

- (for *Square Color Wheel*) Clear tape.

You should definitely try each problem before assigning it in order to decide how many blocks you want to have available.

Description

Much like the *Build It* family that appears on page 44, each clue gives some information you can use to build a particular structure.

These are harder, however. They require more unconventional thinking: the logic can be more twisted; the blocks don't always line up straight; and the structures may not stand on their own. We've also tried to vary the setting; in one, for example, the blocks represent parts of rooms in a condo the group designs.

Possible Debriefing Questions

How did these problems compare with the ones from *Build It*?

How were they different?

How did your group solve the problems?

How did you know when you were done?

Did any of the problems have more than one solution?

Cheops

There are fourteen blocks in all, in four colors.

One of the red blocks is directly above the other, but they do not touch.

Cheops

The blocks on each level form a square.

The second level is all one color.

Cheops

None of the four yellow blocks touches another yellow block.

The top block sits on four blocks in the next level down.

Cheops

Each blue block shares full faces with two yellow blocks.

Each red block touches four green blocks.

Cheops

At least one vertex (corner) of every block coincides with the center of another block's face.

Some blocks have five of these vertices.

Cheops

Each blue block shares an edge with two other blue blocks.

Each yellow block shares an edge with a red block.

from *Get It Together* • EQUALS, Lawrence Hall of Science

What's Next?

Yellow is not next to Red.
Blue is not next to purple.
Red is not next to orange.

Build the row of six blocks

What's Next?

Purple is not next to yellow.
Blue is not next to orange.
Green is not next to red.

Build the row of six blocks

What's Next?

Orange is not next to yellow.
Green is not next to blue.

Build the row of six blocks

What's Next?

Green is not next to yellow.
Purple is not next to green.

Build the row of six blocks

What's Next?

Blue is next to yellow.

Build the row of six blocks

What's Next?

Orange is next to green.

Build the row of six blocks

Box of Cubes

There are 27 cubes in all. Just one layer of the box has Red cubes and it is made up of all Red cubes.

Build the box!

Box of Cubes

When all the Reds are on the bottom of the box a Blue shows up on all of the other sides.

Build the box!

Box of Cubes

There are 12 Green cubes. There are no Blue cubes on any of the corners or edges of this box.

Build the box!

Box of Cubes

You can't see any Yellow cubes no matter how you turn the box, but Yellow is one of the colors of cubes.

Build the box!

Box of Cubes

There are three more Green cubes than Red cubes in this box—and just 5 Blue cubes.

Build the box!

Box of Cubes

Only four colors of cubes are used to make this box.

Build the box!

from *Get It Together* • EQUALS, Lawrence Hall of Science

Square Color Wheel

There are six blocks in all, all different colors.

Build it — but if you do it with blocks alone, it will fall apart. We recommend clear tape.

Square Color Wheel

The primary colors are red, blue, and yellow. Each primary-colored block shares an edge with the other two primaries.

Build it! Use your clue to help your group.

Square Color Wheel

Every block in the structure shares a face with two and only two others.

Use your clue to help your group build it!

Square Color Wheel

Each secondary color (green, purple, or orange) shares faces with the two primary colors that you mix to get it.

Help your group build it!

Square Color Wheel

Blue and yellow make green. Yellow and red make orange.

Build it — but if you do it with blocks alone, it will fall apart. We recommend clear tape.

Square Color Wheel

If you look at the secondary colors, each block shares an edge with the other two. So the green block shares one edge with the orange and one with the purple, and so forth.

from Get It Together • EQUALS, Lawrence Hall of Science

Foofie's Condo

Foofie the Glork's condo has a red stairwell. Use two red blocks, one on top of the other.

Two bedrooms—which do not share a wall—are blue, so represent them with blue blocks.

Foofie's Condo

There are seven blue blocks in the condo, and seven orange. The living room is green.

The condo's two bathrooms and the stairwell are the *only* rectangular rooms in the building.

Foofie's Condo

The kitchen and one of the bedrooms are orange, and the bathrooms—one block each—are yellow.

Your group's job is to use blocks to design Foofie the Glork's condo.

Foofie's Condo

Three bedrooms, one bathroom, and the top half of the stairwell are upstairs; everything else is downstairs—including the six green blocks.

The outside shape of Foofie's condo is a rectangular box.

Foofie's Condo

It's easier for plumbers—and cheaper   if the bathrooms are on top of each other. Make sure that's the case.

By the way, where's the front door? It should open into the living room.

Foofie's Condo

Be sure you can get into each bedroom from the stairwell, and that you don't have to go through the kitchen to get upstairs.

There are twenty-four blocks in all in your model of Foofie's condo.

from *Get It Together* • EQUALS, Lawrence Hall of Science

Measurements

Concept Areas

Measurement, different units, converting between units, imprecision in measurement, gasoline mileage, weight, volume, displacement, nonstandard units, distance, cost.

For Each Group:

- Paper and pencil.

Description

This is a diverse family of problems. Each clue gives an essential piece of a problem that involves measurement—but what is being measured could be weight, cost, volume, or length, depending on the problem.

Features

Where the *Polygons* family (page 62) required students to measure in order to draw something exactly, these story problems are more about the principle of measurement, especially the ideas that you can use different units to measure the same thing (paces or feet or inches), that you can use nonstandard units

(beans for weight instead of grams), and that you can use measurement and units to find out other related quantities (you can translate volume into weight and mileage into cost).

Both actual measurement (using scales or rulers or watches) and understanding of the meaning of units of measurement are essential for our students. Knowing about the cost, size, mass, or duration of something is vital for understanding how it works. Again, traditionally underserved groups need these background experiences in order eventually to have access to higher-level courses that will lead to more satisfying jobs.

Possible Debriefing Questions

If you measure the same thing over and over, will you always get the same answer?

About how much does your desk weigh? Can you figure it out without weighing it?

Do you know how much you can lift? Does it matter how it's shaped?

About how big is an acre?

How much does it cost to operate a typical car in cents per mile? For gas only? How about including insurance and maintenance?

How long is your stride? How would you measure it?

How would you measure the distance to the ceiling if you can't reach it?

Park Perimeter

Luis helped his friends by pacing off two sides of the park: Third Street and Columbus. It took him 120 paces. What's the perimeter of the whole park?

Lupe is as tall as Luis but walks normally. Her pace is 30" long.

Park Perimeter

Lupe paced off the Fourth Street, Maple Street, and Third Street sides of the park. She needed 192 paces. What's the perimeter of the whole park?

Luis's little sister Lonnie is the smallest. Her pace is only 24".

Park Perimeter

When Lawrence helped his friends pace off the park's perimeter, he took Fourth Street and Columbus Avenue. He needed 96 paces to do the two sides. His stride is shorter than Luis's, who was really trucking at 36" per step.

Park Perimeter

The four friends were trying to measure the distance around the park. Each paced off some of the park's four sides.

Lonnie paced off Maple and Fourth. She took 120 paces.

Lawrence's stride is 30" long.

Park Perimeter

The Third and Fourth Street sides of the park are parallel, but the other two are not.

This park is too small to fit a full-size soccer field.

Park Perimeter

When the four friends got home, they realized that they had enough information to draw an accurate map of the park even though they had only set out to measure the perimeter. Can your group do it?

from *Get It Together* • EQUALS, Lawrence Hall of Science

The Length of the Class

Marcia used a meter stick (over and over again) to measure the length of the classroom. She found that it was 12 meters and 30 centimeters long.

How long is the classroom?

The Length of the Class

Giovanni measured the length of the classroom and found that it was 12.25 meters long. (He used a yard stick and converted to meters when he was done.)

How long is the classroom?

The Length of the Class

Edgar measured the length of the classroom and found that it was 11.38 meters long. (He used a meter stick over and over again.)

How long is the classroom?

The Length of the Class

Tiffany measured the length of the classroom and found that it was 12.41 meters long. (She used a metric tape measure.)

How long is the classroom?

The Length of the Class

Salvador measured the length of the classroom with a twelve-inch ruler; he found it was 40 feet 8 inches long.

How long is the classroom?

The Length of the Class

Eleanor measured the length of the classroom with a metric tape-measure; she found that the classroom was 12.45 meters long.

How long is the classroom?

Beans 'n' Boxes

The beans in the green box weigh as much as the beans in the other two boxes put together.

How many beans are in each box? And how much does each box weigh empty?

Beans 'n' Boxes

The blue box—with its beans—weighs twice as much as the red box empty.

This problem has more than one solution. If there are fewer than fifty beans altogether, how many solutions can you find?

Beans 'n' Boxes

The red box and its beans weigh the same as the green box empty.

No beans have been broken in this problem; they're all whole beans.

Beans 'n' Boxes

One quarter of all the beans are in the red box.

The blue box—empty—weighs half as much as the beans in the red and green boxes together.

Beans 'n' Boxes

The number of beans in each box is even.

The collection of beans from the green box weighs more than the red box does empty.

Beans 'n' Boxes

In every box, the beans weigh less than the box.

Furthermore, the green box and its contents weigh more than all of the beans put together.

from *Get It Together* • EQUALS, Lawrence Hall of Science

MGB MPG

Emily Knobloch drives a white MGB. Every fortnight she puts nine gallons of gasoline in her tank to fill it up.

Emily is planning a one-hundred-mile trip. How much will the gasoline cost?

MGB MPG

Where Emily lives, gas for her car costs $1.08 per gallon.

An MGB is a British-made sports car. Emily's MGB handles really well, but it's often in the shop.

MGB MPG

Ordinarily, the only driving Emily does during the week is her trip to work and back, which she does five times a week. That round trip is fifteen miles.

A fortnight is two weeks, by the way. Fourteen days.

MGB MPG

Every weekend she drives to see her friend Charlotte Lucas. That's her only driving on the weekend (she takes her bicycle the rest of the time). The round trip to Charlotte's is six miles.

MGB MPG

How much will the gas cost for Emily's trip? If you knew the price of gas and how many miles Emily's MGB goes on a gallon of gas, you could figure out the cost of driving one mile.

MGB MPG

Emily is very unusual in that she drives fewer than 5000 miles per year. But how much will gas cost for her trip?

It might help to figure out how many miles per gallon (MPG) Emily's car gets.

from *Get It Together* • EQUALS, Lawrence Hall of Science

Rooda and Stooda

Rooda and Stooda are identical twins. They got into their hot tub, which is a cylinder one meter in diameter. One meter is 100 cm.

How much does Rooda weigh?

Rooda and Stooda

When Rooda and Stooda got into their hot tub, it was filled to the top with water.

Though they were careful and didn't splash, a lot of water spilled out; when they got out, the top of the water was ten centimeters down.

Rooda and Stooda

At one point, Rooda and Stooda were both completely under water. After that, no more water spilled out.

By the way, one liter is 1000 milliliters or 1000 cubic centimeters.

Rooda and Stooda

Like most people, Rooda and Stooda barely float. That means that the weight of the water they displace is about the same as their own weight.

One liter of water weighs one kilogram.

Rooda and Stooda

You're supposed to find Rooda's weight in kilograms. It's less than 50. Is that reasonable? Figure out Rooda's weight in pounds, too.

One kilogram is about 2.2 pounds.

Rooda and Stooda

The area of the surface of the hot tub is πr^2, where π (pi) is 3.14... and r—the radius—is half the diameter.

The twins' last name is Baker, by the way.

from *Get It Together* • EQUALS, Lawrence Hall of Science

Constructions

Concept Areas

Geometry. Formal constructions using the language of angles, congruence, similarity, and so forth. The Pythagorean theorem and special triangles.

For Each Group:

- Paper and pencil

- Compass

- Straightedge

- Protractors and calculators

The Geometric Supposer (computer software) is an intriguing alternative.

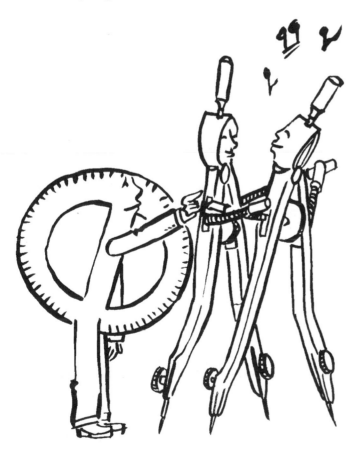

Description

These problems are most appropriate for high-school geometry, but they are accessible to junior high students with adequate preparation. Each problem asks the group to find some measurement in a geometrical construction. Each clue helps the group complete the drawing from which the answer must be taken. A typical clue might be, "line segment AB is tangent to circle C at its midpoint."

For easier geometry problems, see *Stick Figures* (page 50) or *Polygons* (page 62).

Geometry frightens many of us away from mathematics forever. Here, the group setting is the key. These problems give students a chance to use mathematical language with a purpose. If a student doesn't know what "tangent at the midpoint" means, the group will puzzle it out together. Students don't have to feel stupid, and because they are all working to solve the problem—and because they get to see it in a picture when they're done—it's more likely to stick.

Other Comments

Some students continue with their original drawing rather than redraw it, even when they decide on measurements for segments that make their construction terribly out of scale. For example, an isosceles triangle might turn out on the drawing to be radically scalene. In spite of that, students arrive at correct answers and don't seem to be bothered by a drawing that can't possibly represent what they say it does. So a good *individual* assignment at the end of one of these problems might be to make a good drawing of the figure that led to the solution.

Possible Debriefing Questions

What does the figure look like, really? Have different groups draw it on the board. Compare and contrast.

Are there different diagrams that are both right?

Which clues were most useful in these problems?

The Length of $\overline{AB}$

$\triangle ABC$ is a right triangle (though $\angle ABC$ may not be a right angle).

Your job, as a group, is to figure out the length of segment $\overline{AB}$.

The Length of $\overline{AB}$

DCAB is a rectangle.

$\angle DCB$ is the same size as $\angle CBA$.

The Length of $\overline{AB}$

Line segment $\overline{BD}$ is four inches long.

$m\angle DCB + m\angle BCA = 90°$.

"$m\angle DCB$" means, "the measure of angle DCB," that is, its size in degrees.

The Length of $\overline{AB}$

The length of $\overline{BC}$ is five inches.

$\angle BAC$ is a right angle.

Draw a picture to help your group solve the problem.

The Length of $\overline{AB}$

The perimeter of $\triangle BDC$ is twelve inches.

Your job, as a group, is to figure out the length of segment $\overline{AB}$.

The Length of $\overline{AB}$

The area of $\triangle ABC$ is six square inches.

$\overline{AB} \parallel \overline{CD}$.

from *Get It Together* • EQUALS, Lawrence Hall of Science

Radius of Circle C

Line $\overleftrightarrow{RT}$ is tangent to circle C at S.

Point R is *not* on circle C.

Your group's job is to find the radius of circle C.

Radius of Circle C

Line $\overleftrightarrow{PR}$ is tangent to circle C at Q.

Circle C is the only circle in the problem, and C is the name of the point at its center.

Your group's job is to find the radius of circle C.

Radius of Circle C

The measure of angle QRS is 60°. Don't forget that your group should draw a picture.

Your group's job is to find the radius of circle C.

Radius of Circle C

Line segment CR is 12 cm long, and $\overleftrightarrow{CR} \perp \overleftrightarrow{PT}$.

Your group's job is to find the radius of circle C.

Radius of Circle C

The distance from R to S is half the distance from R to P.

Your group's job is to find the radius of circle C.

Radius of Circle C

Line segment QT intersects line segment PS at C. It will help to draw a picture.

Your group's job is to find the radius of circle C.

from *Get It Together* • EQUALS, Lawrence Hall of Science

Sector ACF

Segment CE is 10 cm long.

Sector ACF is part of a circle whose center is C. What is the area of sector ACF?

Sector ACF

Line segment AE is a diameter of the circle whose center is point C.

What is the area of sector ACF?

(A sector of a circle is shaped like a part of a pie; it's bounded by an arc and two radii.)

Sector ACF

Point F is on the circle with center C. There is only one circle in this problem.

What is the area of sector ACF?

Sector ACF

The length of segment EF is the same as the length of segment AC.

What is the area of sector ACF?

Sector ACF

Sector FCE has half the area of sector ACF.

Don't forget that your group should draw a picture!

What is the area of sector ACF?

Sector ACF

The area of the whole circle is pi ($\pi = 3.14\ldots$) times the square of the radius.

Also remember that the sum of the angles on the inside of a triangle is 180°.

What is the area of sector ACF?

from *Get It Together* • EQUALS, Lawrence Hall of Science

In ∠ JAM

There is always one circle that passes through any set of three non-collinear points. But there is only one.

JKLM is a rhombus.

Some problems in life (and math) have extra information that doesn't help you answer the question.

In ∠ JAM

A rhombus is a parallelogram with no right angles whose sides all have equal length.

The sum of the interior angles of a triangle is 180°.

m∠ JMK = 45°.

In ∠ JAM

The measure of the angle subtended by a chord of a circle from any point on that circle is half the measure of the intercepted arc.

m∠ MKA = 60°

What is the measure of ∠ JAM?

In ∠ JAM

A chord of a circle is a line segment with both endpoints on the circle.

Point A is on the circular arc defined by points M, L, and K.

Draw a picture to help solve the problem.

In ∠ JAM

The perpendicular bisector of a chord goes through the center of the circle.

K, A, and the midpoint of $\overline{JL}$ form the vertices of an equilateral triangle.

What is the measure of ∠ JAM?

In ∠ JAM

m∠ LAK = 135°; m∠ KJL = 45 °; and m∠ JLA = 75°.

The measure of a circular arc is the angle subtended by that arc as seen from the center of the circle.

What is the measure of ∠ JAM?

© 1989 The Regents of the University of California
from *Get It Together* • EQUALS, Lawrence Hall of Science

FLAG Day

ΔFGH is a right triangle, but G may not be the vertex of the right angle.

What is the area of quadrilateral FLAG?

FLAG Day

Points J and H trisect line segment $\overline{FA}$, and J bisects $\overline{AH}$.

What is the area of quadrilateral FLAG?

FLAG Day

HG = AJ = 5 cm.

What is the area of quadrilateral FLAG?

FLAG Day

Point H is the midpoint of $\overline{GL}$.

What is the area of quadrilateral FLAG?

FLAG Day

The distance from A to L is $\sqrt{125}$ cm

What is the area of quadrilateral FLAG?

FLAG Day

ΔAJL has the same area as ΔFHL.

What is the area of quadrilateral FLAG?

from *Get It Together* • EQUALS, Lawrence Hall of Science

Number Patterns

Concept Areas

Sequences of numbers. Finding the next number in the pattern. Students also use algebra to relate the numbers to one another.

The problem *Feeding Frenzy* (page 137) has an attribute common to several of the more advanced problems: there is more than one solution without the optional clue; the optional clues make the solution unique. Chances are students will come up with the unique solution anyway, but in case they don't, be prepared with a good question or two.

For Each Group:

- Manipulatives.

- Pencil and paper.

Description

Each problem has a sequence of numbers. Groups need to figure the sequence out. In some problems, the clues relate members of the sequence to one another ("The third number is twice the second number plus one."). You might think of solving the problem as if it were algebra, and then trying to figure out the pattern based on the results. Other problems are more situational in nature, depicting a situation where a number pattern arises naturally.

Whichever way the problem is set up, these are multiple-step problems ideal for groups. As with the *School Math* problems (page 76), the group has to hold a lot of different ideas simultaneously.

Features

Once the numbers in the sequence are established, the group still has to figure out its rule! Extending sequences is a classic problem that appears in all sorts of math tests. More important, extending sequences can help students deepen their understanding of functions. The idea of a function is central to mathematics from algebra on and is vital to success in a math-based career.

Possible Debriefing Questions

Which patterns were harder to figure out?

Which was easier—finding the numbers in the patterns or figuring out how to extend the patterns?

What sort of strategies did your group use to extend the patterns?

If you extend a pattern, how do you know if you are right?

Pattern-o-Piles

The second pile has one-fifth as many as the fifth pile.

There is only one in the first pile.

If the pattern continues, how many are in the sixth pile?

Pattern-o-Piles

The second pile has half as many as the third pile.

If the pattern continues, how many are in the sixth pile?

Pattern-o-Piles

The fourth pile is one third less than the fifth pile.

If the pattern continues, how many are in the sixth pile?

Pattern-o-Piles

If you put the first, second and third pile together, you would get the fourth pile.

If the pattern continues, how many are in the sixth pile?

Pattern-o-Piles

If the piles were people, each pile would have a good number for making a human pyramid. (One person is a small pyramid.)

If the pattern continues, how many are in the sixth pile?

Pattern-o-Piles

The fourth pile is the third pile plus four.

If the pattern continues, how many are in the sixth pile?

from *Get It Together* • EQUALS, Lawrence Hall of Science

What's the Pattern?

The sixth number is the third number times four and it is the first number times eight.

What is the seventh number in the pattern?

What's the Pattern?

The third number is the second number plus one, and the fourth number is the third number plus one.

What is the seventh number in the pattern?

What's the Pattern?

The fifth number is the third number plus the fourth number.

What is the seventh number in the pattern?

What's the Pattern?

When you add the first six numbers together, the sum is twenty.

What is the seventh number in the pattern?

What's the Pattern?

The third number raised to the third power equals the sixth number.

What is the seventh number in the pattern?

What's the Pattern?

The first and second numbers are the same.

What is the seventh number in the pattern?

Annabelle Arable

Annabelle Arable was a successful farmer and landowner. She started out with only ten acres of land in the year after the Big Drought.

What year was the Big Drought?

Annabelle Arable

Annabelle Arable was so successful that after every fall harvest, she bought all the fields that shared a fence with her own.

Those other farmers left Cakewalk County for the Big City to seek their fortunes.

Annabelle Arable

In Cakewalk County, where Annabelle lived, each field is perfectly square and shares a fence with the four fields that surround it. Each field is also exactly ten acres.

Annabelle Arable

In the summer of 1914, Annabelle had 410 acres of land.

When was the Big Drought in Cakewalk County?

Annabelle Arable

Every year, Annabelle Arable's total landholdings were in the shape of a square (sort of), though she never held a square number of acres or fields.

By the way, there are 640 acres in a square mile.

Annabelle Arable

In May 1915, at the age of seventy-three, Annabelle retired.

She gave 200 acres to each of her three children and kept ten for herself, where she raised prizewinning asparagus for many years.

from *Get It Together* • EQUALS, Lawrence Hall of Science

The Bus Stops Here

A city bus with forty-five seats picks up its first passenger at First Street.

The Bus Stops Here

The bus picks up its second passenger at Second Street.

Once all the seats are filled, people have to stand. In what block do people start having to stand?

The Bus Stops Here

Starting with Third Street (the third stop), the number of people who get on the bus is equal to the sum of the boarders from the previous two stops.

The Bus Stops Here

Everyone who gets on the bus gets off three blocks after they get on.

The Bus Stops Here

If everyone got off after two blocks instead of three, the number of riders when the bus pulled up would be the same as the number of people waiting for the bus at each stop.

The Bus Stops Here

There are six people in the bus between Fourth and Fifth streets.

Two people get off at Sixth Street.

from *Get It Together* • EQUALS, Lawrence Hall of Science

Feeding Frenzy

Bugwumps are usually very sweet, but every two months, in the middle of the night, they go on a feeding frenzy and devour trundles as quickly as possible.

On May 1, 1934, there were thirty-six Trundles.

Feeding Frenzy

During the first month after a feeding frenzy, the Trundles quadruple in population.

Here's the question: How many Trundles were there on the morning of January 1?

Feeding Frenzy

During the night the Bugwumps feed, they gobble up five out of every eight Trundles.

This problem takes place between January 1 and May 1 of the year 1934.

Feeding Frenzy

During the second month following a feeding frenzy, the population of Trundles doubles.

The Bugwump feeding frenzies always occur during the night preceding the first day of a month.

Feeding Frenzy

The Bugwumps ate twenty Trundles during the frenzy on the night of February 28, 1934.

No one had ever seen a Bugwump (or a Trundle, for that matter) until late December, 1933.

Feeding Frenzy

There were three times as many Trundles on April 1, 1934 as there were on February 1.

No one has ever figured out how Bugwumps know when the first day of the month is.

from *Get It Together* • EQUALS, Lawrence Hall of Science

Find the Function

Concept Areas

Analytic geometry. Official mathematical $f(x)$-type functions: lines, a parabola, a circle, and a rectangular hyperbola.

For Each Group:

- Graph paper.

- Scratch paper and pencil.

- Compass and straightedge.

Possibly computer graphing software or a graphing calculator.

Description

These problems, for Intermediate Algebra, Analytic Geometry, Precalculus, or beyond, use concepts like intercepts and slope. They require students to recognize and reproduce equations for common functions. A typical clue might be, "this function has a slope of one where it crosses the y–axis."

As far as we know, each of the problems has only one solution.

Purpose

Understanding the connection between equations and graphs is esential for students who want to continue in math beyond Geometry. While some students catch on immediately, others take a while to become comfortable with this connection and with the idea of a function. The more varied opportunities we give students for solving these problems, the better—and the more different ways of approaching them we can show them, the more flexible and resilient they will become.

Other Comments

As students move into more stratospheric mathematics, it's vital that we keep presenting opportunities for cooperative learning. Too often we get overwhelmed with how much we have to teach, how much content there is. The result might be that our students get overwhelmed as well, and the ones we most need to help can drop out because math is no longer required. Problems like these are only the tip of what you can do, but they are a start.

Possible Debriefing Questions

What types of clues were most useful?

What places did you get stuck?

Numbers one and two are both lines. Which one was easier? Why?

Point A lies on the line $y = 1$.

Find the equation for the line that contains points A and B.

The x-coordinate of point A is the negative of the y-coordinate of point B.

Find the equation for the line that contains points A and B.

Point B lies on the line $y = 2x$.

Find the equation for the line that contains points A and B.

The x-coordinate of point B is twice the y-coordinate of point A.

Find the equation for the line that contains points A and B.

The slope of this line is 1/2.

Find the equation for the line that contains points A and B.

The line never passes through the fourth quadrant.

Find the equation for the line that contains points A and B.

from *Get It Together* • EQUALS, Lawrence Hall of Science

Find the Function 2

Line l intersects the line segment that connects point Q to the origin.

Your group should write the equation for line l and draw its graph.

Find the Function 2

Line l has an x-intercept of –2.

Help your group write the equation for line l and draw its graph.

Find the Function 2

Point Q is at (–3, –3). But point Q is not on line l.

Write the equation for line l and draw its graph.

Find the Function 2

The closest line l comes to the origin is the square root of two units away.

Your group should draw a graph of line l and write its equation.

Find the Function 2

Line l never passes through the first quadrant. Based on this clue alone, what can you say about its slope?

Your group's job is to write the equation for line l and draw its graph.

Find the Function 2

Point Q is $\sqrt{10}$ away from line l's y-intercept.

Your group's job is to write the equation for line l and draw its graph.

Find the Function 3

This function is a second-degree polynomial—a parabola.

Use your clue to help your group figure out its equation and draw the graph.

Find the Function 3

This function's slope is zero where it passes through (1,2).

Use your clue to help your group figure out its equation and draw the graph.

Find the Function 3

The graph of this polynomial passes through the origin. You can write this equation as a polynomial in x.

Use your clue to help your group figure out its equation and draw the graph.

Find the Function 3

The graph of this function passes through (3, -6).

Use your clue to help your group figure out its equation and draw the graph.

Find the Function 3

If you write the function as a polynomial, x has a coefficient of 4.

Use your clue to help your group figure out its equation and draw the graph.

Find the Function 3

This function has two real roots: 0 and 2.

Use your clue to help your group figure out its equation and draw the graph.

from *Get It Together* • EQUALS, Lawrence Hall of Science

Find the Function 4

The graph of this relation is tangent to the x axis.

Use your clue to help your group figure out its equation and draw the graph.

Find the Function 4

This is not really a function at all—it's a relation. In fact, it's a circle.

Use your clue to help your group figure out its equation and draw the graph.

Find the Function 4

This graph passes through (-3, 10) and (0, 1).

Use your clue to help your group figure out its equation and draw the graph.

Find the Function 4

The two points where this graph intersects the positive y-axis are eight units apart.

Use your clue to help your group figure out its equation and draw the graph.

Find the Function 4

This figure is mostly in the second quadrant, and not at all in the fourth.

Use your clue to help your group figure out its equation and draw the graph.

Find the Function 4

This figure has an area of 25π.

Use your clue to help your group figure out its equation and draw the graph.

from *Get It Together* • EQUALS, Lawrence Hall of Science

Find the Function 5

This function is a rectangular hyperbola shaped like y = 1/x.

Use your clue to help your group figure out its equation and draw the graph.

Find the Function 5

This function is undefined for x = −1.

Use your clue to help your group figure out its equation and draw the graph.

Find the Function 5

There is no value of x for which $f(x) = 1$—but all other values are in the range of f.

Use your clue to help your group figure out its equation and draw the graph.

Find the Function 5

The slope of this function is 1 where it passes through the origin.

Use your clue to help your group figure out its equation and draw the graph.

Find the Function 5

The slope of this function is positive everywhere it is defined.

Use your clue to help your group figure out its equation and draw the graph.

Find the Function 5

As x approaches $+\infty$, $f(x)$ approaches 1 from below.

Use your clue to help your group figure out its equation and draw the graph.

from *Get It Together* • EQUALS, Lawrence Hall of Science

Wodjah & Co.

Concept Areas

Algebra. Word problems from more complex situations, including probability and physics.

For Each Group:

- Paper and pencil.

- Manipulatives.

Note: *B, G, & E* and *Metro Gnome* require all six clues. Check the blips.

Description

These are complex word problems. They vary considerably in their subject matter and in how to solve them. All of the problems yield to persistence and common sense. Here the fact that a group is working on the problem often makes it tractable. Using the Jigsaw technique we describe on page 75 may make these problems more accessible to middle-school students.

In this family, the multiple-step problems of the *School Math* (page 76) and *Kids With Stuff* (page 28) families have grown into maturity. These problems are very rich; each could easily take a high-school class period with discussion. At the same time, they can be solved by ambitious middle-schoolers. It depends what tools you bring to bear.

Our goal is to provide opportunities for multiple-step problem solving in complex situations where traditionally underserved students—or just those that do poorly—tend to give up. Debriefing after the problems—always a good idea—is essential with problems like these. Students need to describe how they solved the problems in order to look into the process of their own learning. We want them to make that process explicit, not just get the right answers.

Other Comments

If you're working with older students, you may get some resistance to using manipulatives. Do your best to overcome it, perhaps by introducing them with much easier problems (like those in *Kids With Stuff* or *Number Shapes*) first. In debriefing, be sure to talk explicitly about the advantages and disadvantages of using symbolic algebra as opposed to manipulatives. We want to use whatever strategy works the best. For some problems, algebra is most efficient; for others, blocks work faster—even for someone fluent in *x*s and *y*s.

Possible Debriefing Questions

Where did you get stuck?

How did you get un-stuck? What did the group do to help?

Were there any advantages to working with a group in these problems?

Your Guide Wodjah

When you met your guide Wodjah at the Regina Maris Port of Entry, he took you to currency exchange, where you got 29 Reggies in the form of a red bill (called a "redback"), a blue one, a black one, and a yellow.

"Oh, goody," said Wodjah, you got one of every kind of bill we have!"

Your Guide Wodjah

Your guide Wodjah bought you a postcard for one Reggie. He handed the storenik two yellowbacks and received three reds in change.

"We have no one-Reggie bill here on Regina Maris," he explained.

Your Guide Wodjah

When Wodjah bought you a cheap ceramic lizard as a souvenir, he gave the storenik two bluebacks and got three yellows in change.

Here is your group's problem: What is the value (in Reggies) of each of the different colored bills on Regina Maris where Wodjah works?

Your Guide Wodjah

Wodjah had to break a blackback. The banknik behind the counter gave him a blue and a yellow.

"I should get you a cheap ceramic lizard," he said, "It's a traditional gift for visitors to Regina Maris. Only costs one Reggie."

Your Guide Wodjah

"There are no numbers on the money," you said to Wodjah, "how do you know how much a bill is worth?"

"You'll figure it out," he said, "for example, if you have exactly two bills, you can't have two, three, five, or twenty Reggies."

Your Guide Wodjah

On Regina Maris (a small island vacation spot with knowledgeable native guides like Wodjah) the paper money — Reggies — is printed on different-colored bills.

The four colors are black, red, yellow, and blue, each a different denomination.

B, G, and E

In January, according to B, G, and E, Basil and Cecily used 200 kWh of electricity and 60 therms of gas.

How many therms did they use in October?

What's a therm? It's a unit of natural gas energy. They bill you for them. The more you use, the more you pay.

B, G, and E

Cecily and Basil Splinterwaithe were billed £50.00 in July by B, G, and E.

They use natural gas for heating—the furnace and the water heater—and electricity for lights and appliances.

How much do they pay B, G, and E in a year?

B, G, and E

In July, the Splinterwaithes were billed for 150 kWh and 20 therms.

Their bill in October was £72.

What is the cost per kWh? That is, what does B, G, and E charge its customers for one kWh of electricity?

B, G, and E

kWh stands for "kilowatt-hour," a measure of electrical energy. The more you use, the more they charge you.

Cecily and Basil used 180 kWh in April.

Every one of the six cards in this set has a question. Here's yours: which questions can be answered exactly?

B, G, and E

Basil and Cecily Splinterwaithe have a comfortable home in Surrey. Their bill from B, G, and E in January was £100.00.

Most of the petroleum deposits under the North Sea are natural gas, not oil.

What was the Splinterwaithe's April bill from B, G, and E?

B, G, and E

B, G, and E (British Gas and Electric, a fictitious government-owned utility made private by the Thatcher government) billed Cecily and Basil for 50 therms of natural gas in April.

£ is the symbol for pounds. That's British money. £100 means, "100 pounds."

What is the price of one therm of natural gas from B, G, and E?

from *Get It Together* • EQUALS, Lawrence Hall of Science

Metro Gnome

Zbig is very small and lives in a big city. Even though he is 117 years old, they think he's a kid, so they sent him to PS 12962.

Your job, as a group, is to calculate the approximate speed of sound (in feet per second) based on Zbig's experiences. Remember: there are sixty seconds in a minute.

Metro Gnome

When Zbig is **at** recess, the band practices Sousa marches (like The Stars and Stripes Forever) with the bandroom window open onto the playground. Zbig sometimes claps along with the music, one clap on every beat. He stands right by the tetherball pole.

Draw a picture to help solve the problem!

Metro Gnome

Every Sousa march is marked (by the composer) to be performed at a tempo of one hundred twenty beats per minute.

In spite of difficulties, the band director at PS 12962 always keeps the tempo.

Metro Gnome

Zbig noticed that when he claps, he can hear the reflection of the claps coming back at him from PS 12962's unremarkable concrete façade. When Zbig claps along with the Sousa marches, the reflections of the claps arrive just as he is clapping the very next clap.

Draw a picture to help solve the problem!

Metro Gnome

Remember, Zbig is very short! He can walk right under turnstiles, sure, but if you walk with him, he probably has to take about two steps for every one of yours. In fact, he can walk only 15 feet in ten steps.

Draw a picture to help solve the problem!

Metro Gnome

The distance from the tetherball pole to the concrete façade is 180 lonely Zbig-steps. It's lonely because of a scheduling mixup: even though there are five hundred kids in the fourth grade, Zbig has recess alone.

from *Get It Together* • EQUALS, Lawrence Hall of Science

Who's on Twenty-First?

There's this list, see. Use your clue to help your group figure out the twenty-first item on the list.

Each odd-numbered item (starting with the third) is the sum of the previous two.

Who's on Twenty-First?

There's this list, see. Use your clue to help your group figure out the twenty-first item on the list.

Each even-numbered item (starting with the fourth) is the difference between the previous two odd-numbered items.

Who's on Twenty-First?

There's this list, see. Use your clue to help your group figure out the twenty-first item on the list.

The sum of the first four items on the list is three.

Who's on Twenty-First?

There's this list, see. Use your clue to help your group figure out the twenty-first item on the list.

All of the items on the list are integers. None are less than zero.

Who's on Twenty-First?

There's this list, see. Use your clue to help your group figure out the twenty-first item on the list.

The eighth item is the same as the sixth.

Who's on Twenty-First?

There's this list, see. Use your clue to help your group figure out the twenty-first item on the list.

Most odd-numbered items are larger than the even-numbered items that follow them.

from *Get It Together* • EQUALS, Lawrence Hall of Science

Loaded Dice

On the red die, one of the numbers comes up half the time. The other five numbers are equally likely.

In 100 rolls of the red and blue dice together, 8 came up 29 times while 7 came up only 14 times.

Which face is most likely to show up on each die?

Loaded Dice

The red and the blue dice look normal. Each has six faces. But they're both loaded.

In 100 rolls of both dice together, nine came up eight times, and six came up nine.

Which face is most likely to show up on each die?

Loaded Dice

On the blue die, five of the numbers are as likely as one another, but the other one comes up half the time.

There's a red die too; when I rolled the two dice 100 times, 2 came up only once, but 10 came up seven times.

Which face is most likely to show up on each die?

Loaded Dice

The average roll of the blue die alone is greater than that of the red die.

In 100 rolls of both dice together, 3 and 11 each came up six times.

Which face is most likely to show up on each die?

Loaded Dice

Miraculously, in the 100 rolls, the numbers came up exactly as you would expect them from probability. For example, 4 came up 7 times, and 7/100 is the probability of rolling a four.

Which face is most likely to show up on each die?

Loaded Dice

If you had two of the red dice and one blue, and the red dice were loaded the same, you would get about five times as many 18s as 3s.

Which face is most likely to show up on each die?

Restraint

Ask questions whenever possible, and avoid giving strategies or answers for the problems. Group problem solving is an exercise in cooperation for students but one of self-restraint for teachers. Cooperative learning makes the classroom learner- instead of teacher-centered. It gives students authority and responsibility for their own learning. But we teachers usually want to help too much.

We are still in charge. We make the rules, set the direction of the class and create the environment. But to make it work, we have to help the students rely on themselves and one another instead of the teacher.

Giving responsibility to our students and the groups also means being willing to let them do it in their own time. When a group is on a wrong tack, we want to point their way back out of the wilderness. When a group member is disruptive, we want to take care of that so the rest of them can get on with learning. When we have figured out a new rule that would help everybody work more smoothly, we feel like imposing it. When we have had a world-class revelation about our students' thinking, we want to tell them about it. But if they do it themselves, they'll learn it that much better. In general, it's best to keep our hands (and voices!) off.

Some practitioners make the distinction between *intervening* and *interacting* behaviors. The important bit is that intervening solves the problem in the short term but invites it to stick around for next time. An interacting behavior may not solve a problem immediately, but is more likely to solve it permanently.

For example, suppose Michael comes to you while you're observing and asks you what a parallelogram is. The intervening behavior is to tell him. The interactive response is usually a question. The first is, "Is this a group question?" Maybe somebody in the group knows.

If the group is stuck and calls you over—always respond as quickly as possible if there's a group question—you might ask, "What do you think a parallelogram is?" "Do you know which of these Pattern Blocks are parallelograms?" Maybe you know where a parallelogram is drawn in their book. Maybe they should look it up in a dictionary. If they really have no idea, ask them to check with another group. Whenever possible, ask a question. Consider having the class create a wall chart of "Good Places to Look for Information."

Other teacher actions that tend to undermine the autonomy of the groups are: settling arguments, reminding students of the rules, giving tips on the math, and, of all things, praising. Honest. Save it for the debriefing.

Even in the debriefing, try to make it *their* debriefing. You are the teacher, it's yours to guide, but be attentive to their agenda as well. Again, try not to be too quick with adult wisdom. This actually happened:

Teacher:	Who will tell me what it was like doing the problems with the sticks today?
Melissa:	It was hard. Our group took a long time and we only did one problem.
Teacher:	Why was that? What made the problem hard?
Brett:	[Melissa's group] We couldn't figure it out until Steffa read her clue about there being eleven sticks altogether.
Teacher:	Any other group have that problem?
Eve:	We did. But once we knew there were eleven sticks, we got it right away.

Sal:	That was the clue we read first. I guess that was why I thought it was easy.
Melissa:	These problems aren't fair. Sometimes you read the clues in the right order, and if you don't, you get stuck for a long time.
Sal:	That's right. It shouldn't matter so much which order you read the clues in.
Teacher:	What could we do to solve that problem?

At this point, somebody came up with the bright idea that they should all read their clues *before* trying to solve the problem, and start with the best "starter." They discussed which of the clues were good starters, and how to recognize them. They compared the *Sticks* problems to another type of problem and recognized good starters there, too.

It would have been easy for the teacher to start the class by saying, "boys and girls, I want you to take turns reading your clues first; everybody reads before anyone can touch the sticks." By not doing that, not only did the students discover that it was a good idea (not just a rule) but they launched into an analytical discussion about the structure of problems.

Answers

The hardest hands-off technique for many teachers is not giving answers. The group finishes; they all raise their hands for another problem. When you get there, envelope-in-hand, they chorus, "did we get it?"

We tend not to give answers in our classes. True, students need reinforcement and feedback, but see if you can get the reinforcement from the group and from the class. Turn it back to them. "Do you think you're correct?" "What have you done to check?" "Does anyone have any doubts?"

Under what conditions is it better to have the decision on rightness come from the group? Does this apply anywhere outside the math classroom? And what about the crisis of courage that occurs when they call you over and say they've checked their work and they're all convinced but you see that they're wrong? What do you do then? These are important questions, and while it's important to ask them, we don't know all the answers.

It may seem that this has been a long section about how not to do anything: how not to intervene; how not to answer individuals; how not to give answers to problems. Other strategies for keeping your hands off include being sufficiently well-prepared that you can let go and feel in control of the situation (if not of every detail) and giving yourself some behaviors to observe. Most of all, enjoy getting a chance to watch your students and listen to them.

Remember that you're making them independent. The more you succeed, the easier it will be on you, because they'll take more and more responsibility for what they learn.

Around the World

Concept Areas

Descriptive statistics about the world—population, languages, and so forth. Exposure to the world outside the USA.

For Each Group:

- Labels that you will cut from each sheet of clues. Include them in the problem envelopes.

- Paper and pencil.

Description

Each problem presents global statistics about something: the ten largest cities, the ten most widely spoken languages, population density, and so forth. Individual clues help the group put the cities (or whatever) in order. The clues frequently contain unnecessary but interesting side information that helps illuminate the importance of the statistics being discussed.

These problems might best be used as engaging introductions or reinforcements for a set of social-studies lessons. Here, the logic involved is useful but not essential. The important thing is to keep the information in front of the students in a way that can help them make it their own.

Features

This problem format need not be limited to mathematics! And mathematics need not be confined to math period. In this family, we keep the math connection but try to involve students in problem-solving with content that's clearly global.

As our students develop their intellectual tool-boxes, we need to help them use all of their ways of thinking in different settings. If we develop analytical powers, reasoning, teamwork, and the ability to choose appropriate problem-solving techniques in mathematics, but ignore these tools when we try to tackle social problems, we run grave risks. The same is true of the best tools of social science and the humanities: they should be applied in the sciences wherever possible.

Warning

The problem *Newspapers and TVs* demands a more sophisticated reading level, and, like the *School Math* family, requires students to attend to several variables at once.

Possible Debriefing Questions

Did anything you found out surprise you?

What other languages (or cities, etc.) do you think are close to the top ten?

Do you know anyone who speaks Bengali?

What do you suppose are the ten largest cities in the US?

How many TV sets per thousand people do you think there are in the US, based on your own homes?

Largest Cities in 1990

The only two cities in 1990 with a greater population than Tokyo were Mexico City and São Paolo.

By 1990, Rio de Janeiro was the tenth largest city in the world.

Largest Cities in 1990

The five cities with the largest populations were Tokyo, Calcutta, Mexico City, São Paolo, and New York, but not necessarily in that order.

Buenos Aires, at 11.7 million, had about 200,000 more people than Seoul.

Largest Cities in 1990

The five least populous cities in this problem are Bombay, Seoul, Rio de Janeiro, Shanghai, and Buenos Aires, but not necessarily in that order.

New York had a larger population than Seoul or Calcutta, but was smaller than São Paolo.

Largest Cities in 1990

Bombay, with 11.9 million, was larger than both Seoul and Buenos Aires, but smaller than Shanghai. Mexico City had the largest population in the world.

Problem: arrange the ten cities in order from the largest population to the smallest.

Largest Cities in 1990

Seoul, home of the 1988 Summer Olympics, was smaller than Tokyo or New York, but larger than Rio.

Shanghai and Calcutta both had populations about 12 million and were in the middle of the list.

Largest Cities in 1990

There are three cities between São Paolo and Shanghai in size.

New York had the highest population in 1970, but by 1990, three cities surpassed New York's population.

New York	Shanghai	Calcutta	Buenos Aires	Bombay
São Paolo	Mexico City	Rio de Janeiro	Seoul	Tokyo

from *Get It Together* • EQUALS, Lawrence Hall of Science

Languages of the World

Although more people speak Chinese than any other language, very few non-Chinese speak it.

About as many people speak Portuguese as speak Arabic or Bengali.

Languages of the World

About as many people speak Hindustani as speak Spanish.

About 200 million people speak Bengali.

Your group's task is to rank the top ten languages spoken in the world today.

Languages of the World

Japanese and German are each spoken by less than 4% of the world's population.

One per cent of the world's poulation is roughly equal to 50 million people.

Languages of the World

Russian and Spanish, both spoken by about the same number of people, are very popular languages. Only two— English and Chinese—are spoken by more.

Languages of the World

We believe that the people of the world speak about 5000 different languages.

While English is the official language of India, Hundustani and Bengali are very common languages there. And more Indians speak Hindustani than Bengali.

Languages of the World

Most of the world's roughly 200 million speakers of Portuguese live in Brazil.

Attempts have been made to devise international languages—such as Esperanto—that are easy to learn and to speak, but they have not caught on.

Spanish	Russian	Portuguese	German	Arabic
Bengali	Chinese	Japanese	English	Hindustani

from *Get It Together* • EQUALS, Lawrence Hall of Science

Population Density

Population density is the number of people per square mile.

The USSR and South America have population densities only 3 people per square mile different from North America's.

Population Density

North America has a population density five times Australia's.

Europe and Asia (omitting the USSR) have the same poulation density: nine less than six times Africa's.

Population Density

Africa has ten more people per square mile than North America.

The USSR has the second lowest poulation density. **Problem:** Find the population densities of the seven areas mentioned in this problem.

Population Density

Australia has the smallest poulation density — only seven people per square mile.

If you leave out the USSR, Asia and Europe are the most densely populated continents on Earth.

Population Density

Though they have large populations, North America and the USSR have lower population *densities* than South America and Africa because of the huge amounts of cold, virtually uninhabitable land area in Northern Canada and in Soviet Asia.

Population Density

The most crowded country is Bangladesh, where the high fertility of the land supports a large rural population.

The difference between the highest and lowest densities is 254 people per square mile.

North America | South America | Europe (w/o USSR) | USSR | Asia (w/o USSR) | Australia | Africa

from *Get It Together* • EQUALS, Lawrence Hall of Science

Energy Consumption

North America uses ten times as much energy as South America, and twelve times as much as Africa.

What percentage of the world's energy supply does each of the seven regions use?

Energy Consumption

The USSR alone uses only 1% less of the world's energy supply than the rest of Asia together.

What percentage of the world's energy supply does each of the seven regions use?

Energy Consumption

Oceania—that's Australia, New Zealand, and a lot of Pacific island nations—uses half as much energy as all of South America. But put Oceania with Asia and Africa, and together they use as much as all of Europe without the USSR.

Energy Consumption

Asia (without the USSR) uses eight times as much energy as Africa. South America uses 3% of the World's supply.

What percentage of the world's energy supply does each of the seven regions use?

Energy Consumption

Europe (without the USSR) uses eight times as much energy as South America and sixteen times as much as Oceania.

The percentages you figure out should add to 100%.

Energy Consumption

The USSR, Africa, and Oceania together use as much energy as Asia and South America.

Africa uses the least amount of energy per person of all the regions in this problem.

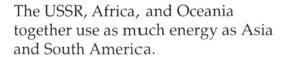

North America | South America | Europe (w/o USSR) | USSR | Asia (w/o USSR) | Oceania | Africa

© 1989 The Regents of the University of California   from *Get It Together* • EQUALS, Lawrence Hall of Science

Newspapers and TVs

A thousand average people from the USA have six times as many television sets as the same number of Brazilians.

About twice as many newspapers are printed every day—per 1000 people—in Brazil than in India.

Newspapers and TVs

Indians print about seven times as many newspapers daily than they have televisions. In contrast, the Japanese have only a few more daily newspapers printed than they have TV sets.

Which country has the most TV sets per one thousand people?

Newspapers and TVs

In Brazil, there are three times as many televisions as daily papers. Even so, there are a little more than four times as many TV sets per 1000 people in Japan than in Brazil.

Which country prints the most newspapers per 1000 people? How many?

Newspapers and TVs

There are a little more than twice as many newspapers per thousand people in Japan than in the USA.

There are only about three TV sets for every thousand people in India.

All of the numbers in this problem are per 1000 people.

Newspapers and TVs

Most industrialized countries have 300 to 400 TV sets per 1000 population.

Newspapers and TVs

There are about 800 telephones per thousand people in the USA. That's still more than the number of television sets.

| U S A | Brazil | Japan | India |

from *Get It Together* • EQUALS, Lawrence Hall of Science

Back to Nature

Concept Areas

The idea that organisms live in the environments to which they are best adapted. Whale families, life on mountains and in the salt marsh. The effects of temperature and altitude.

For Each Group:

- Only materials from this book.

Note: three of the problems require a separate page where students place the answer pieces.

Also: all of these problems require all six clues; there are no "optional" clues in this family!

Description

Students get clues about parts of an environment or particular organisms. The group has to put the information together to decide which organisms live where. The first problem is somewhat different; here we're compiling information about the sizes of whales.

Features

As we saw in the family *Around the World*, problems in this form don't have to be strictly mathematical. Here we move into the natural world and study the interaction of organisms with their environments.

These problems are ideal if you are planning or have just been on a field trip to the area in question. But they are also useful as springboards for *any* discussion of habitat and adaptation.

The last two problems, *Where Do They Live?* and *Where Do They Grow?* are about the same regions—but one is about animals and one is about plants. The two are related. Doing *Grow* first will help the students.

Possible Debriefing Questions

Why do you suppose those different plants live at different altitudes?

Why do the different salt marsh organisms live at different levels?

Have you ever seen a jackrabbit? A whale? A marsh hawk? Jeffrey pine tree?

If you look at plants around your school, can you think of why some of them live where they do? For example, where does grass grow? And where doesn't it grow?

Whale Lengths

The bowhead whale is 20 feet shorter than the fin whale.

The whales (order Cetacea) have two suborders, the baleen whales and the toothed whales.

Whale Lengths

A one-week-old baby blue whale is as large as a pickup truck.

A full-grown fin whale is about 20 feet shorter than a full-grown blue whale.

Use the information on this card to help your group solve the problem.

Whale Lengths

A mature blue whale measuring 100 feet has a heart as big as a Volkswagen (a beetle, not a van).

No one knows for sure how many species of whales there are, but scientists estimate there may be 80 to 100 different species.

Whale Lengths

The largest toothed whale is 63 feet long.

A full-grown gray whale is half the size of a full-grown blue whale.

Use the information on this card to help your group solve the problem.

Whale Lengths

A sperm whale (the kind in *Moby Dick*) can dive to 10,000 feet and stay underwater for 90 minutes.

The maximum lengths of the bowhead whale and the sei whale are about the same.

Whale Lengths

All whales that grow to 50 feet or more are baleen whales except one, the sperm whale, which is a toothed whale.

Here is your group's problem: how long is each of the six species of whale when it is fully grown?

Sperm Whale

Bowhead Whale

Sei Whale

Blue Whale

Gray Whale

Fin Whale

from *Get It Together* • EQUALS, Lawrence Hall of Science

The Salt Marsh

Runners of salt grass lay a dark green carpet on the mud above the upper boundary of pickleweed.

The marsh hawk has a white rump patch and feeds on mice and other small animals that cross the dry grasslands to nibble on saltbushes and juicy pickleweed.

The Salt Marsh

Pickleweed grows nearer the high tide mark than alkali heath and its string of gray-green "pickles" are actually fleshy leaves fused together around the central interior stem.

Copepods swim in the waters of the salt marsh.

Use your information to help your group put the labels on the right places on the mat.

The Salt Marsh

Although pickleweed can tolerate having its roots in wet mud, it cannot tolerate long periods of submergence.

On the other hand, cordgrass can endure many hours of submergence; it dominates the mid-tide zone.

Use your information to help your group put the labels on the right places on the mat.

The Salt Marsh

Cordgrass is the pioneering plant of the salt marshes and is one of the most productive plants in the world, yielding up to eight tons of dried material per acre.

The largest wading bird of the salt marshes is the Great Blue Heron, standing four feet high with a seven-foot wingspread.

The Salt Marsh

Sometimes a few spikes of cordgrass get a start in the saltgrass, but most cordgrass grows below the high tide line.

Pickleweed is the dominant plant of the average high-tide level, growing about 18 inches tall.

Use your information to help your group put the labels on the right places on the mat.

The Salt Marsh

Alkali heath and other halophytes grow in the uppermost level of the intertidal zone, where the highest tides wet the soil only a few times a year.

The marsh hawk hunts from the sky, gliding along on its four-foot wingspan.

from *Get It Together* • EQUALS, Lawrence Hall of Science

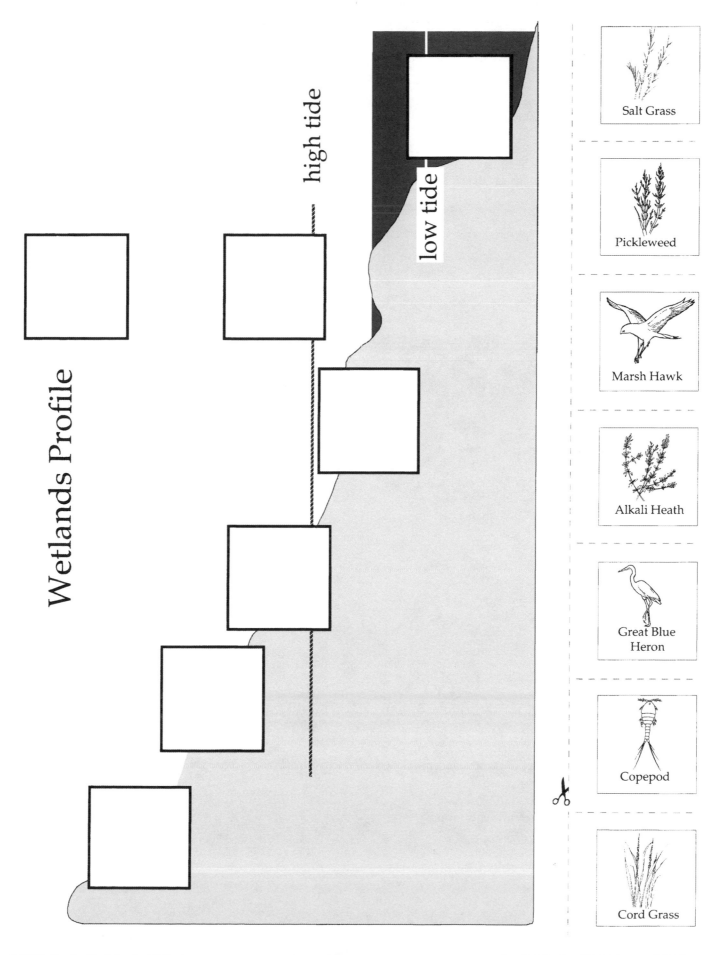

Wetlands Profile

high tide

low tide

Salt Grass

Pickleweed

Marsh Hawk

Alkali Heath

Great Blue Heron

Copepod

Cord Grass

from *Get It Together* • EQUALS, Lawrence Hall of Science

Where Do They Grow?

The height, steepness, temperature, moisture, and other characteristics of the land influence the species that live there.

Ranchers raise cattle and sheep in the shadscale shrub area between 3000 and 6000 feet elevation.

It gets colder and the growing season gets shorter, the higher you go.

Where Do They Grow?

No trees, only small plants grow in the alpine fell fields, a harsh environment with ferocious winds, rocky soil, and thin air.

The mixed coniferous forest has a great variety of trees in broad canyons with 30-60 inches of precipitation and a growing season of 2 1/2 to 3 1/2 months.

Where Do They Grow?

Plants can be grouped according to the communities where they are usually found.

Whitebark pine grows in broad glacial basins, near the high mountain lakes and the rocky ledges of the subalpine forest where the growing season is 7 to 9 weeks.

Where Do They Grow?

The Jeffrey pine can grow to 180 feet tall. Its needles come in threes, and it thrives where the growing season is about three months.

The bright blue sky pilot grows far above the Jeffrey pine in a place of heavy snow, gale-force winds, and a growing season of only 4 to 7 weeks.

Where Do They Grow?

Mojave rabbitbrush and bitterbrush grow in areas where deer are plentiful.

The lodgepole pine and the whitebark pine share the same areas as the alpine columbine and the foxtail pine.

Use your information to help your group put the plant labels on the right places on the mat.

Where Do They Grow?

The desert snowberry grows above the Mojave rabbitbrush in an area that gets some snow and has a growing season of five to eight months.

Cattle and sheep graze on spiny hopsage in an area with heavy soil and warm air—but limited water.

© 1989 The Regents of the University of California.

from *Get It Together* • EQUALS, Lawrence Hall of Science

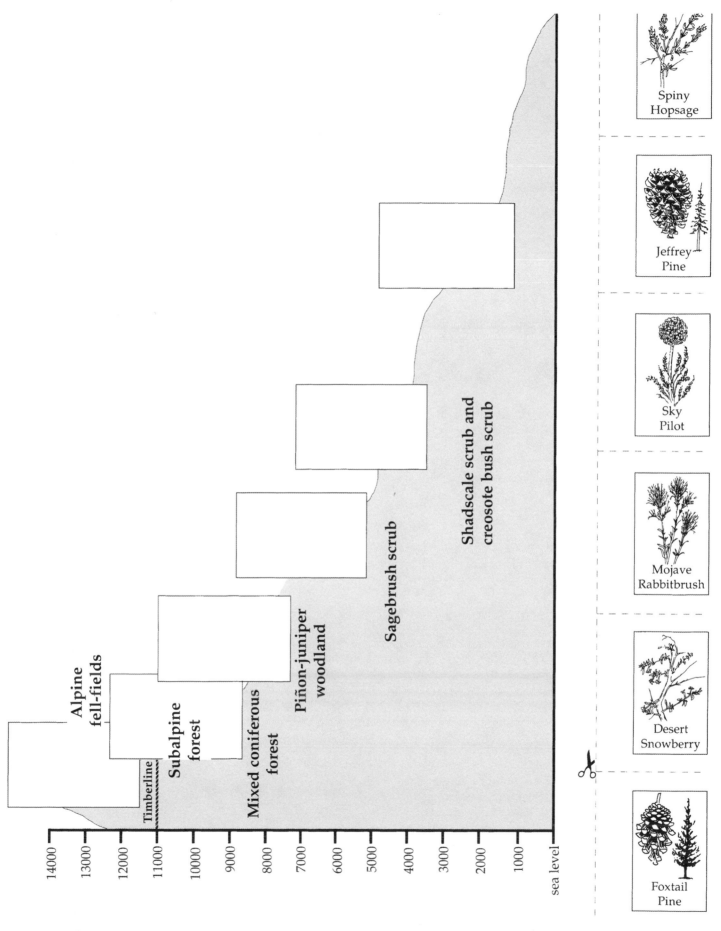

Alpine
fell-fields

Timberline

Subalpine
forest

Mixed coniferous
forest

Piñon-juniper
woodland

Sagebrush scrub

Shadscale scrub and
creosote bush scrub

14000
13000
12000
11000
10000
9000
8000
7000
6000
5000
4000
3000
2000
1000
sea level

Spiny
Hopsage

Jeffrey
Pine

Sky
Pilot

Mojave
Rabbitbrush

Desert
Snowberry

Foxtail
Pine

from *Get It Together* • EQUALS, Lawrence Hall of Science

Where Do They Live?

The porcupine ranges widely, but prefers forests such as lodgepole pine and fir.

In the Alpine Arctic zone, snow covers the ground to a depth of 40 or more feet and lasts seven to nine months.

Find the preferred zone for each animal.

Where Do They Live?

Canadian Zone trees include a two-needled pine called "Lodgepole" and two species of fir tree, the red and the white firs.

The black-tailed jackrabbit lives in a zone much lower than the pika.

Find the preferred zone for each animal.

Where Do They Live?

The Jeffrey pine forests are in a zone immediately below the Lodgepole pines.

The white-tailed antelope squirrel is able to live in the open desert prairie country where temperatures are very high. It does not live in any higher, cooler zone.

Find the preferred zone for each animal.

Where Do They Live?

The least chipmunk eats seeds, grains, and the greenery it finds in the Jeffrey pine forest.

The Sierra marmot lives in the highest mountains. Marmot signs have been found on the top of a 13,000 foot peak.

Where Do They Live?

The hot desert of the lower Sonoran zone is suited to prairie plants such as spiny hopsage.

The pika spends its short summer cutting and collecting stems of plants such as alpine columbine. It leaves this "hay" to dry, and then gathers it into a protected area for use during the long snowy winter.

Find the preferred zone for each animal.

Where Do They Live?

The pika (also called "cony" or "rockrabbit") lives in the high rock slides near the timberline.

Black-tailed jackrabbits can leap two or three yards at a bound, touching only their toes to the high desert ground.

Find the preferred zone for each animal.

from *Get It Together* • EQUALS, Lawrence Hall of Science

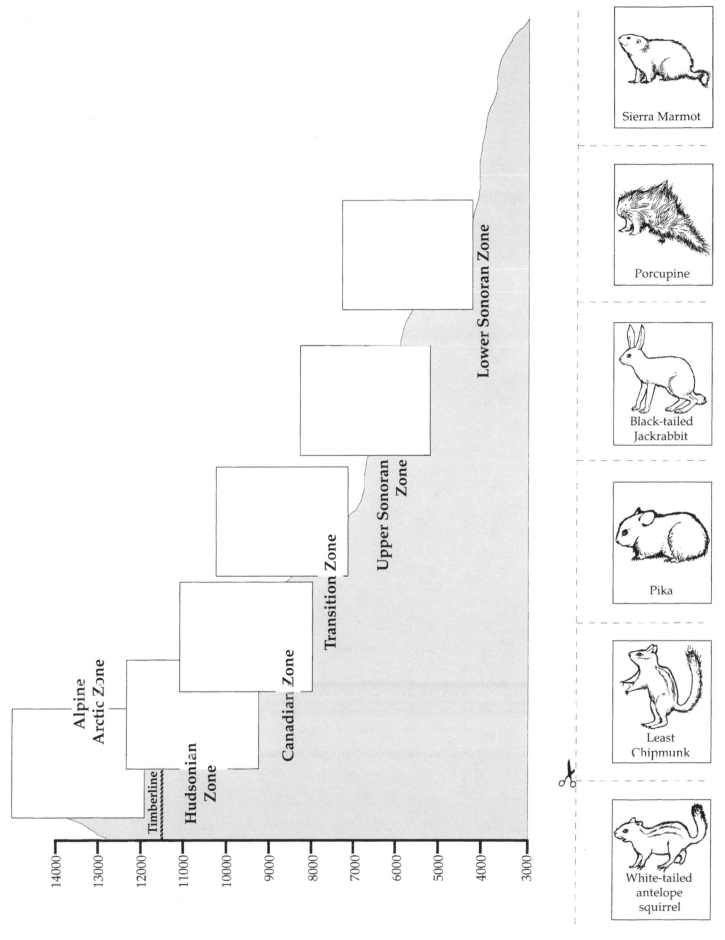

Alpine Arctic Zone

Timberline

Hudsonian Zone

Canadian Zone

Transition Zone

Upper Sonoran Zone

Lower Sonoran Zone

14000 13000 12000 11000 10000 9000 8000 7000 6000 5000 4000 3000

Sierra Marmot

Porcupine

Black-tailed Jackrabbit

Pika

Least Chipmunk

White-tailed antelope squirrel

from *Get It Together* • EQUALS, Lawrence Hall of Science

Martian for Beginners

Concept Areas

Logic. Recognizing patterns and organizing information. Language: parts of speech, sentence structure, comparatives, verb tenses, and a lot more.

For Each Group:

- Paper and pencil.
- A good memory.
- A sense of humor.

Note: these problems may require all six clues from any of the previous problems.

Description

A Martian lands at the UN building in New York and you're in charge of talking with it. Unlike a typical Sci-Fi movie alien, it speaks only Martian. Fortunately, your clues are scraps from the *Berlitz Martian-English Dictionary* and the *Comparative Martian-English Grammar*. Your group has to decipher the Martian's utterances and prepare appropriate responses. Who knows what might happen if you succeed?

Besides the unusual subject matter, this family has one more attribute unique to this book: each problem requires information from previous problems' clues. Therefore, students need access to all previous clues (including the clues that were optional at the time). *It is very important that students not see the next problem until they have solved the current one!*

Features

These problems build on one another. Again, we try to take our mathematical skills outside the traditional math curriculum; again, we try to invade another discipline, though we're sure there are no Martian specialists teaching classes in your district.

As with many of the problems in this book, this set has a social message. This family is about cultural differences and suspending our expectations of people (and others) we might meet. While we don't expect this ulterior message to have much effect in one application, it's important to take these small steps as often as possible. You might say that changing the way our society views other cultures (like changing the way we use language to avoid sex stereotypes) is like basting a turkey. Let's leave it at that.

Possible Debriefing Questions

Have you ever been somewhere where everyone spoke a language you didn't understand?

Did you enjoy these problems? Were they frustrating?

How did you organize the Martian vocabulary? When you needed to remember a word, how did you do it?

If you took a book and translated it from English to Martian, would it be longer or shorter? Why?

1. The Landing

A Martian lands on top of the United Nations Building in New York, its first words are **zu hemohap**.

What is it saying?

1. The Landing

From the *Comparative Martian-English Grammar*:

Sentence type	English	Martian
Declarative	Ends in .	begins with **zik**
Interrogative	Ends in ?	begins with **zu**
Exclamatory	Ends in !	begins with **ziz**

1. The Landing

Selected nouns from the *Berlitz Martian-English Dictionary*:

parent	**mricta**
job	**toba**
peace	**hemo**
cloak	**repup**
spacecraft	**soza**
nucolator	**zictscha**

1. The Landing

From the *Comparative Martian-English Grammar*:

The suffix **hap**, when appended to a noun root, converts that noun to an adjective. Unlike English, a given noun can have one and only one adjective. For example, **zik bo mrictahap** means, "he is fatherly," or "she is motherly."

1. The Landing

From the *Comparative Martian-English Grammar*:

In Martian, if a sentence has no verb, you should assume the verb "to be" in the present tense. For example, **zu bo mricta** means, "Is it a parent?"

1. The Landing

From the *Comparative Martian-English Grammar*:

Martian sentences don't need to have a subject when they are addressed to a group. So "You are dirty" can be shortened to "dirty." In Martian, the sentence is **zik yunhap**, where **zik** is the word that introduces a declarative sentence.

from *Get It Together* • EQUALS, Lawrence Hall of Science

2. The Reply

Your delegation wants to reply to the Martian. You want to say,

"Yes, we are peaceful."

How will you do that?

2. The Reply

From the *Comparative Martian-English Grammar*:

Conjugation of the verb "to be"

Person	Past	Present	Future
I	zoot	zook	zood
you	zoot	zook	zood
he/she/it	zoot	zook	zood
we	zooter	zooker	zooder
they	zooter	zooker	zooder

2. The Reply

From the *Comparative Martian-English Grammar*:

Affirmative sentences in Martian end in **kal**. Sentences without **kal** at the end can be ambiguous, or even interrogative. Thus, "yes, it is a parent" would be, **zik bo mricta kal**.

2. The Reply

From **mapokolor**'s *Quick Guide to Conversational Martian*: A Martian bends its body in the middle when it replies to a question. For a human, this would look like a bow.

From the *Comparative Martian-English Grammar*, the pronouns:

I	**e**	we	**er**
you	**doe**	you [all]	**doer**
he/she/it	**bo**	they	**boer**

2. The Reply

From the *Comparative Martian-English Grammar*:

Negative sentences in Martian end with the word **lak**. This corresponds roughly to English sentences beginning with "no."
Thus, "no, it is not a parent," would be **zik bo mricta lak**.

2. The Reply

Selected adjectives from the *Berlitz Martian-English Dictionary*:

dirty	**yunhap**
warlike	**galdhap**
happy	**sillerhap**
old	**zirkhap**

from *Get It Together* • EQUALS, Lawrence Hall of Science

3. Necessities

On hearing your pronouncement, the Martian says, **zik er zooker hemohap; ziz e rook zolomohap yantek**, and its body begins shaking.

What should you do?

3. Necessities

From the *Comparative Martian-English Grammar,* some sample sentences:

I love you!	**ziz e mook doe**
Do you love me?	**zu doe mook e**
I will need food.	**zik e rood zudistch**
I feel warm.	**zik e keek zilomohap**
We want a blue spacecraft.	**zik er djooker trud soza**

3. Necessities

From the *Comparative Martian-English Grammar,* prefixes and suffixes modifying nouns and adjectives:

dirt	**yun**	happiness	**siller**
a bit dirty	**ziyunhap**	content	**zisillerhap**
dirty	**yunhap**	happy	**sillerhap**
filthy	**zoyunhap**	joyful	**zosillerhap**

3. Necessities

Selected nouns from the *Berlitz Martian-English Dictionary:*

toilet	**wo**
heat	**lomo**
room	**glog**
water	**yantek**

3. Necessities

Selected verbs from the *Berlitz Martian-English Dictionary:*

want	**djoo**
need	**roo**
feel	**kee**
give	**ba**
have	**poo**

all of the above verbs are conjugated like **zoo** (to be).

3. Necessities

Not all Martian adjectives are created from nouns. Selected adjectives from the *Berlitz Martian-English Dictionary:*

near	**paq**	red	**gaad**
far	**mak**	good	**gad**
blue	**trud**	shiny	**kriz**

from *Get It Together* • EQUALS, Lawrence Hall of Science

4. More Necessities

You hand a tea kettle of boiling water to the Martian, who, to your horror, pours it all over itself. But not a drop reaches the ground—and the shaking stops. The Martian then says, **zu zook woglogen ropaq zlip**. What now?

4. More Necessities

From the *Comparative Martian-English Grammar*, note the Martian question words **zu-marp**, **zu-zlip**, **zu-morp**, and **zu-glin** and the word order they require:

What time is it?	**zu zook trup marp**
Where was I?	**zu zoot e zlip**
Who are you [all]?	**zu zooker doer morp**
Which book is best?	**zu zook tok rogad glin**

4. More Necessities

From the *Comparative Martian-English Grammar*, note the comparative forms of Martian adjectives:

good	**gad**	old	**zirkhap**
better	**regad**	older	**rezirkhap**
best	**rogad**	oldest	**rozirkhap**

4. More Necessities

From the *Comparative Martian-English Grammar*, plurals and articles in Martian and English:

book	**tok**	job	**toba**
the book	**token**	the job	**toban**
books	**toker**	jobs	**tobar**
the books	**tokener**	the jobs	**tobaner**

4. More Necessities

From the *Comparative Martian-English Grammar*, combining roots:

zlipzill =	zlip + zill	
	location for person	= house
glogfoo =	glog + foo	
	room for sleep	= bedroom
toktidma =	tok + tidma	
	book for heart	= diary
zillzlip =	zill + zlip	
	person for location	= navigator

4. More Necessities

From the *Comparative Martian-English Grammar*, combining roots:

Names in Martian always begin with **ma**. A Martian has only one name, which may or may not be derived from those of its three parents. Possessives are constructed using the adjective suffix **hap**, as in **zu zooter makalahap mrictar morp** — Who were Makala's parents?

from *Get It Together* • EQUALS, Lawrence Hall of Science

5. sozahap zillener

zik zilltoken marookipahap
mricta

zu zill glin pook zu toba glin

5. sozahap zillener

zik matapa zook rozirkhap

zu zill glin pook zu toba glin

5. sozahap zillener

zik zillsozan rezirkhap
marcoshpa

zu zill glin pook zu toba glin

5. sozahap zillener

zik marookipa bat zillzlipen gad
gaad repup
ziz zillzlipen zosillerhap

zu zill glin pook zu toba glin

5. sozahap zillener

zik zillzlipen bat matapa kriz
zictshan

zu zill glin pook zu toba glin

5. sozahap zillener

zik zillsozan pook zictscha lak

zu zill glin pook zu toba glin

from *Get It Together* • EQUALS, Lawrence Hall of Science

Making New Problems

Not all of the problems in this book will be useful to you and your classes or your families. They may be too hard, or too easy. Or you may just want more. Make your own—or have your students do so! You'll understand these problems better—and your students will understand the material better—the more you and they create your own.

Let's talk about inventing problems like these. First, you need an *appropriate* problem—one that is amenable to group solution. Once you have it, you need to make up good clues, that is, clues that genuinely contribute without giving the whole thing away. And how do you make sure that the problem is soluble with the right number of clues?

In general, our problems require four clues and have two optional clues. That's a pretty good recipe, but hard to make work sometimes. (For example, in our *Number Shapes* family, since there are only three numbers to be found, we can't require more than three clues without introducing another shape!) How did we make our problems work? There are two answers: plenty of trial-and-error, and plenty of field-testing. We can't possibly describe all of the specific thinking we used to create these problems, but we can give you some strategies for creating your own.

If some of your problems don't work, don't panic. In real problem-solving you have to cope with insufficient or out-of-whack information. You may be doing your students a favor!

Modifying existing problems

The easiest technique is to take a problem you like and change it. We've done that ourselves in the *Small City Block* family, where there are four problems that are structurally identical. We've done more than simply change the names, though; in some problems we've changed directions as well. That means we still had to test the problems carefully in case we accidentally changed the way you solve the problem by changing the details.

Translating the Problems

One way to create new cooperative math problems that you might not immediately consider is to translate them into another language. The next page has Lynne Alper's Spanish translation of *Two Kids with Animals*. (The English version is on page 29.)

Niños y Animales

Cada niño tiene el mismo número total de animales (cuando se suma el número de cerdos y pollos.)

¿Cuántos cerdos tiene Ronaldo?

Niños y Animales

Los animales de Alejandra tienen todos juntos dos patas más que los animales de Ronaldo.

¿Cuántos cerdos tiene Alejandra?

Niños y Animales

Los animales de Ronaldo tienen doce patas.

¿Cuántos pollos tiene Ronaldo?

Niños y Animales

En total, los dos niños tienen tres pollos. El resto de los animales son cerdos.

¿Cuántos pollos tiene Alejandra?

Niños y Animales

Ronaldo tiene el mismo número de cerdos y pollos.

Alejandra no tiene el mismo número de cerdos y pollos.

Niños y Animales

Si Alejandra le diera a Ronaldo un pollo, los animales de ella trendrían doce patas en total.

Hay cuatro preguntas que deben ser contestadas por el grupo.

Ronaldo

Alejandra

Problems from Another Source

Find a problem you like and cut it up—writing the information on different clue cards. This has some pitfalls. The first is that most problems don't have four pieces of information that are both interesting and essential! Some problems just don't work cut up. But traditional solve-with-a-chart logic problems like those in puzzle books usually work, as well as some others. Consider this one:

> Monica went to the electrical store to get some supplies. With the $20.00 she took, she bought a pair of pliers, a switch, an outlet, a double outlet-box, and two Romex connectors. The pliers were $12.99, the switch and the outlet were 98 cents each, and the Romex connectors were 32 cents each. She paid $1.25 in tax, at 7%. How much was the outlet box?

This one is rich enough to split up. Important for the problem structure is that there are many steps to the solution and many separable bits of information. Try it! The facing page has a blank problem for you to copy and fill up.

What's Important About Monica

That problem about Monica is unusual in a number of ways: first, it has an equity message. The cooperative version could include career information, adding color to the clues by explaining what these things are used for—maybe even drawing pictures. Second, the question we ask at the end isn't the one you might have expected when you started the problem (probably either "how much altogether?" or "how much change?"). Third, it has extraneous numerical information. Fourth, though it *sounds* like a regular math problem, there are multiple solutions. All of these attributes make this a good problem to use with a group, even though it doesn't touch on unusual parts of math.

Extending a family

Another way to make up new problems is to find a family of problems you like in this book and make up new members. Decide if you want to start with the answer or some of the clues.

For example, in the *Build It*s or in *Stick Figures*, we tended to start with the answer. First we'd build a structure that had some interesting attributes; then we'd try to come up with clues. There are exceptions, however. In *Square Color Wheel* (page 108), we knew we wanted clues about mixing colors, so we built the "colouroboros" solution to that problem with that in mind.

If you have a particular concept you'd like to reinforce, try finding a related family and designing a problem or two around the concept. For example, if you're interested in subsets, the *Venn Family* (page 74) is a good one. There's only one problem in that family that has genuine subsets in it; you could design more. In that case, start with an answer—one that includes subsets—and think up your clues. If you want to study primes under 100, make a problem like those in *Hundred Chart Hunts* where some clue uses a prime.

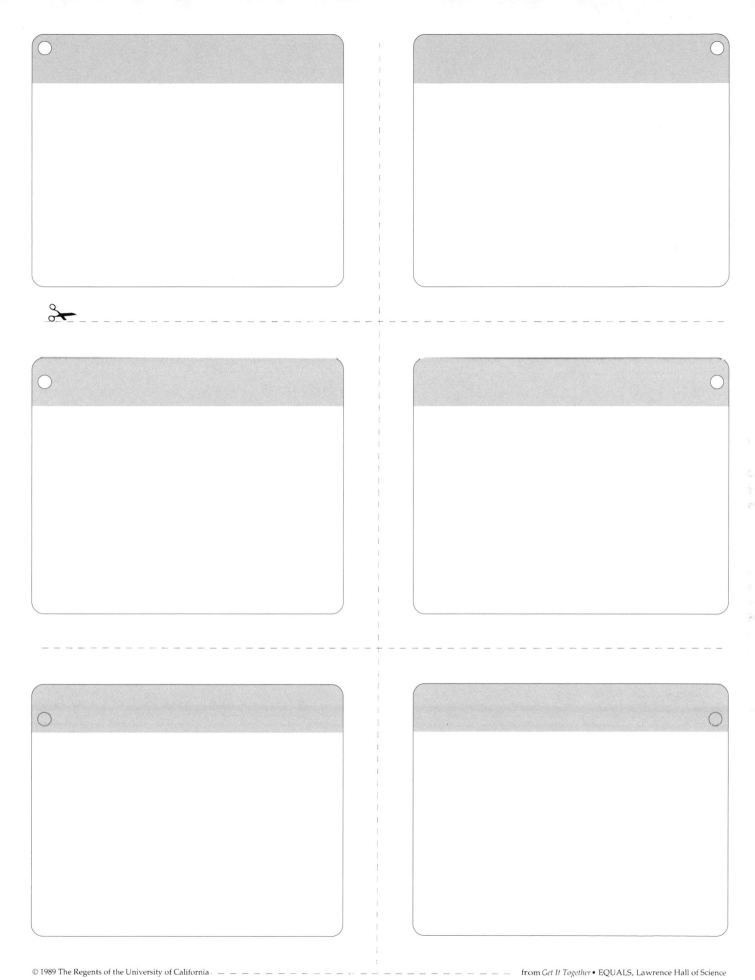

from *Get It Together* • EQUALS, Lawrence Hall of Science

Making a new family, related to an old one

We have some explicit and implicit assumptions in our families. For example, all of the *Stick Figures* solutions are plane figures; all of the solutions to *Kids With Stuff* use whole numbers. You can throw away these assumptions and create a new family.

Imagine, taking off from *Sticks*, a set of problems that use cardboard squares and equilateral triangles as faces of polyhedra. Clues link them, as in "four equilateral triangles come together at two of the vertices of this solid."

Suppose you're teaching Chemistry and you like the *Mysteries* set. Make a set of your own that are really qualitative analysis problems. "When you add weak sulfuric acid to solution A, a bright yellow precipitate forms. Call the yellow solid B and the remaining solution C."

In the process of making up a problem, make sure you don't lose sight of what the problem is supposed to be about. Suppose you're designing something about probability, taking off from *Draw the Spinner*, for example. It's too easy to make it a problem that's really about number patterns instead of probability. But if you combine numbers ("You can get a four in two spins") or refer to events ("…equally likely…" "spinning three is twice as likely as…") you are really dealing with combinatorics and the probability side of mathematics.

Making a "totally" new family

This is the most exciting, of course, and the hardest. There isn't a lot of advice we can give you, except:

- Try modifying old problems and extending families so you get used to their structure from a designer's point of view.

- Remember that not all types of problems fit into this format.

- Brainstorm ideas, considering both ideas for types of clues and ideas for material you want to get across.

- Try to think up new ways you can break up what's necessary to solve a problem.

- Even though you're making up the problem, you should still try to solve it with a small group before you use it in a class!

- Don't be upset if your new type of problem doesn't work. About one in three of our ideas eventually pan out!

Don't be afraid to break out of the mold that made this book. For example, we expect the students to stay more or less at tables and use traditional math manipulative equipment. That needn't be so! Imagine a measurement problem to figure out how many pingpong balls would fit in the classroom. One group member might have a clue to measure the length of the room; another might estimate the height to the ceiling; a third might measure a pingpong ball, and so forth.

Another assumption we make in this book is that the groups are small. Yet we've seen a teacher invent a cooperative problem that involved the whole class. There's no limit! Try anything—and if it works, please let us know!

Resources

Johnson, David W., Roger T. Johnson, Edythe Johnson Holubec, and Patricia Roy. 1984. *Circles of Learning: Cooperation in the classroom*. Alexandria, Virginia: Association for Supervision and Curriculum Development.

This is a short booklet by some of the Big Names in research and practice in cooperative learning. Two of the key phrases are *positive interdependence* and *individual accountability*. The Johnsons are also explicit about teaching social skills necessary to work together. The booklet gives an overview of the research and one model of implementing cooperative learning in the classroom, written mostly for supervisors. For a more detailed account, see their *Learning Together and Alone*, published in 1975 by Prentice-Hall.

Slavin, Robert E. 1982. *Cooperative Learning: Student teams*. Washington, D. C.: National Education Association.

Robert Slavin, from Johns Hopkins, is another of the Big Names. This booklet briefly describes several cooperative learning methods he has promoted, including Student Teams-Achievement Divisions (STAD) and Teams-Games-Tournament (TGT). In these methods, the hope of group rewards motivates individuals within a framework of individual accountability. This booklet is an informative overview; if you want more, get his book, *Cooperative Learning*, published by Longman in 1983.

Aronson, Elliot, N. Blaney, C. Stephan, J. Sikes, and M. Snapp. 1978. *The Jigsaw Classroom*. Beverly Hills: Sage Publications.

These are the people who invented the official Jigsaw Technique. It's a great idea partly because it's so easy to adapt to different settings. You can think of all of the problems in this book as jigsaw problems— though there are important differences. We talk about this more on page 75.

Cohen, Elizabeth G. 1986. *Designing Groupwork: Strategies for the heterogeneous classroom*. New York: Teachers College Press.

Mark this one *highly recommended*. This work, from the Center for Complex Instruction at Stanford, is a thoughtful, research-based exploration of how students working together can enhance subject-matter learning and prosocial behavior. There is less emphasis on motivating students by promising rewards and more emphasis on equity: how to help all students get the education they deserve.

Dishon, Dee and Pat Wilson O'Leary. 1984. *A Guidebook for Cooperative Learning: A technique for creating more effective schools*. Holmes Beach, Florida: Learning Publications.

This is a how-to book for teachers by two disciples of the Johnsons. It's full of practical suggestions and rules-of-thumb including how to attend to social skills and an excellent section on how not to intervene.

Gibbs, Jeanne. 1987. *Tribes: a process for social development and cooperative learning*. Santa Rosa, California: Center Source Publications.

This is the most radical of the set. The *Tribes* model is practical and visionary. Tribes are permanent groups that become more like families than teams in order to foster prosocial goals broader than simply being able to work together. A *Tribes* classroom is a big commitment with big rewards for yourself and for the students. The book focuses on social skills and group-building activities; student motivation comes fom the positive effects of the group rather than from striving towards group rewards.

Index of Problems

Topics Grid

Legend: ■ = definitely, ▨ = somewhat (D = definitely, S = somewhat)

	Grade Levels	Logic	Number	Geometry	Algebra	Probability	Measurement	Functions	Good Jigsaw?	Good Starter?	Page
Hundred Chart Hunts	4–12	S	D						D	D	16
Find the Number	6–12	S	D						D	D	22
Kids With Stuff	4–12	S	D		D			S	D	D	28
Number Shapes	2–9		D		D				D	D	34
Build It!	4–12	S		D	D					D	44
Stick Figures	4–12	S		D			D		D	D	50
Pattern Blocks	4–12	S		D			D		D		56
Polygons	6–12			D			D		D		62
Small City Blocks	4–12	D		D	D				S	D	68
School Math	7–12	S	D		D			S	D		76
Venn Family	5–12	D	S						D	D	82
Lineup Logic	5–12	D		S							88
Mysteries	7–12	D									94
Which Spinner Is It?	4–12	S	S			D			D	D	100
Draw the Spinner	7–12	S				D			D		106
Build It Again	6–12	S		D							114
Measurements	7–12		D	S	D		D	S	D		120
Constructions	8–12			D			S				126
Number Patterns	8–12	S	D	S	D			D			132
Find the Function	9–12		D	D	D			D	D		138
Wodjah & Co.	7–12		S		D	S		S			144
Around the World	6–12		D		+ social studies				D	D	152
Back to Nature	6–12	D			+ natural history						158
Martian for Beginners	7–12	D			+ language						166

■ definitely   ▨ somewhat